A Play

By
WILLIAM HAUPTMAN

SAMUEL FRENCH, INC.
45 WEST 25TH STREET   NEW YORK 10010
7623 SUNSET BOULEVARD HOLLYWOOD 90046
LONDON   TORONTO

IMPORTANT BILLING AND CREDIT REQUIREMENTS

All producers of GILLETTE *must* give credit to the Author of the Play in all programs distributed in connection with performances of the Play and in all instances in which the title of the Play appears for purposes of advertising, publicizing or otherwise exploiting the Play and/or a production. The name of the Author *must* also appear on a separate line, in which no other name appears, immediately following the title, and *must* appear in size of type not less than fifty percent the size of the title type.

So we might as well build a city here
And we'll call it Mahagonny...
All the world's full of hard work and striving
But down here we'll have fun
All a human being can want
Is not to suffer, but do what he feels like...
And every week here will be seven days away from working
And the big hurricanes don't travel northward this far
Instead all perfectly relaxed
Our men will smoke in rocking chairs while the red sun sets
Then every other day we'll have boxing
Lots of noise and violence, but those fights will be fair

Bertolt Brecht, *Rise and Fall of the City of Mahagonny,*
translated by Michael Feingold

GILLETTE was commissioned by the American Repertory Theatre, Cambridge, Massachusetts, Robert Brustein, Artistic Director; and originally produced there in April, 1985.

GILLETTE had its West Coast premiere in August, 1986, at the La Jolla Playhouse, Des McAnuff, Artistic Director, with the following cast:

Mickey Hollister	Jim Haynie
Bobby Nobis	Campbell Scott
Doreen	Gloria Mann
Booger McCoy	Michael Genovese
Poot	Douglas Roberts
Cathy	Susan Berman
Brenda	Sierra Pecheur
Jeeter	Jere Burns
Jody	Barbara Howard
Sonny	Dean Abston
Leon	Deryl Caitlin

The production was directed by Des McAnuff; set, John Arnone; lights, Richard Riddell; costumes, Susan Hilferty; sound, John Kilgore; music by Cadillac Cowboys (Bill Coover, Tommy Rivers, John Schimmel); production stage manager, T.R. Martin.

A revised GILLETTE was subsequently produced by the American Repertory Theatre in November, 1987, with the following cast:

Mickey Hollister . . . . John Bottoms
Bobby Nobis . . . . Andrew Mutnick
Doreen. . . . . Priscilla Smith
Booger McCoy. . . . . Harry S. Murphy
Poot . . . . Marty Lodge
Jeeter. . . . . Thomas Derrah
Cathy . . . . Pamela Gien
Brenda. . . . . Dawn Couch
Jody. . . . . Bernadette Wilson
Sonny. . . . . Michael Balcanoff
Leon/Chigger . . . . Henry DiJohn

The production was directed by David Wheeler; set, Loy Arcenas; lighting, Howell Binkley; costumes, Catherine Zuber; sound, Stephen Santomenna; music by Donny Brooks; production stage manager, Anne S. King.

CHARACTERS

MICKEY HOLLISTER, age forty, a roughneck all his life

BOBBY NOBIS, a college boy

DOREEN, a local girl

BOOGER MCCOY, a toolpusher in his forties

POOT, his buddy

CATHY, a hooker in her early twenties

BRENDA, a hooker in her thirties

JEETER, a deputy

JODY, not quite twenty, an emotionally disturbed girl on the run from her family

SONNY, her boyfriend, a biker

LEON, a cowboy (doubles as Chigger)

SCENE

The play takes place in and around Gillette, a small northeastern Wyoming town that has boomed with the decontrol of oil prices, the discovery of great deposits of coal, the building of several strip mines in the area.

The sets are simple and, unless specified, have no great naturalistic detail. The details, however, should be real—the Silver Dollar should have a real jukebox, for instance, and a real computer game. The costumes should be well-worn, dirty, and correct for the period.

Exterior scenes are played before backdrops of the landscape around Gillette—a featureless yellow prairie, broken here and there by rolling hills, and a startlingly blue sky.

The time is the late summer of 1981.

GILLETTE

ACT I
SCENE 1

SCENE: Morning in the Silver Dollar Lounge, a bar with sheet iron walls on the outskirts of Gillette. There are two tables downstage, a jukebox, a computer game, and a tiny dance floor. DOREEN is behind the bar, a girl with a Farrah Fawcett hairdo. As the LIGHTS come up, MICKEY and BOBBY enter and cross to the bar.

DOREEN. What'll you have?

MICKEY. A couple of ice cold beers.

DOREEN. You got 'em.

BOBBY. I can't believe we're here.

MICKEY. Just take a look around you, son. Gillette, Wyoming: a real live honest-to-god energy boom town.

BOBBY. If your car had broken down one more time...

MICKEY. Stop bellyaching. It got us here, didn't it?

BOBBY. Yeah, with a big ten dollars between us.

MICKEY. Who cares? Why, we can make a thousand dollars a week here without hardly trying. That's four thousand dollars a month. Forty-eight thousand dollars a year. Big coin.

9

BOBBY. *(slapping his palm) Yeah.*

MICKEY. Enough to buy our freedon, son. Enough for me to go to Alaska, and you to pay off your debts. And we never have to go back to the nine-to-five grind.

BOBBY. I just hope there's lots of girls.

MICKEY. *(indicating DOREEN)* Well, that one's not too shabby.

BOBBY. Now *that's* a real piece of love. Watch me put my moves on her.

MICKEY. Hold up. Flip you to see who goes first. *(Flips coin.)* You lose. *(as DOREEN brings their beers)* Hello, there. I'm Mickey Hollister, and I'm a lover of fun. Who might you be?

DOREEN. Somebody who ain't got time for your bullshit.

MICKEY. Me and Bobby here just come all the way from Amarillo, Texas, for your energy boom.

DOREEN. I hate to tell you, Romeo, but there's something like fourteen thousand other guys who got here first. Gillette used to be nothing but a wide spot in the road. *(crossing back to bar)* Now we got two shopping malls, a Kentucky Fried Chicken, and a Cinema One, Two, and Three.

BOBBY. We're free for the evening. How'd you like to show us the sights?

DOREEN. Know how many times a day I get asked that? There's fifty guys for every girl in this town. Know how they say Bo Derek's supposed to be the only perfect ten? Well every girl in Gillette's a five, just by being here — even if she's on Medicare. Hell, a woman's libber or a herpes carrier would be a seven. And if a girl's got any class at all ... why then I guess she's just got to be a ten. *(looking at BOBBY)* But you *are* sorta cute.

BOBBY. You mean you'll go out with us?

DOREEN. That depends on what you've got to offer me.

BOBBY. Besides ourselves? Like what?

DOREEN. A gram of toot would help.

BOBBY. *(to MICKEY:)* We got any toot?

MICKEY. Not that I know of.

DOREEN. You got any 'ludes? Poppers? Darvons?

MICKEY. We ain't even got a stolen credit card.

BOBBY. But we'll tell you lots of funny stories. Then when we get jobs, we'll come back and take you out in style.

DOREEN. You ain't even got *jobs?* What am I doing even talking to you? I don't waste my time with losers like you. I'm a *ten.*

MICKEY. You don't know what you're missing, honey. We're the last of the free men.

DOREEN. Nothing's free, asshole. *(Moves to the other end of the bar.)*

MICKEY. This don't look too promising.

BOBBY. I was doing just fine. Maybe we should split up.

MICKEY. Split up? Why, you couldn't last five minutes in this town. How do you think you're gonna get a job? You never done an honest day's work in your life.

BOBBY. I have so.

MICKEY. I ain't talking about working for Montgomery Ward. I'm talking about *real* work — the kind you got to get right down next to and get nasty. You ain't a working man, son. Not yet. And it shows.

BOBBY. You're right, Mickey. What am I gonna do?

MICKEY. I'm gonna have to give you lessons.

(BOOGER and POOT Enter, two oilfield workers wearing filthy coveralls and hard hats.)

BOOGER. Give us a couple of beers, Doreen.

POOT. *(as they sit at table)* Heard anything about those guys who got tore up?

BOOGER. *(Bites off plug of chewing tobacco.)* That one lost his hand, but they say he's gonna keep his arm.

POOT. I hate it when guys get tore up like that.

BOOGER. Sons-of-bitches shoulda been more careful.

POOT. You been pushing us pretty hard, Booger.

BOOGER. I been pushing myself, Poot. We got to find them hydrocarbons.

POOT. I just hope we got a well.

BOOGER. We got a well. We're gonna perforate them pay zones, and when we do, we're gonna find oil — not salt water, or gas but good ole one hundred percent American crude. Only thing we got to worry about is finding two more men to work on your shift.

DOREEN. *(bringing their beers)* Now Booger, don't go spitting tobacco juice in my ashtray. Use a cup. *(Gives him paper cup.)*

BOBBY. What do we do now?

MICKEY. Well, if we stick around here, maybe we can get jobs.

BOBBY. *(looking around)* Here?

MICKEY. *(socking him on arm)* Stop looking around like

an idiot! Try to look like a working man.

BOBBY. How?

MICKEY. Stick your thumbs in your pocket. Now lean on that bar like you own it. Pick your nose now and then. *(indicating BOOGER and POOT)* Watch those guys, they've got it down cold.

POOT. What about that guy you beat up? You hears anything him?

BOOGER. He's in the hospital.

POOT. You hit him pretty hard.

BOOGER. He had it coming.

POOT. Yeah, but you didn't have to bust his ribs for him.

BOOGER. Son-of-a-bitch was giving me a funny look.

BOBBY. *(watching BOOGER and POOT)* Jesus Christ, what if I get in a fight with one of these guys? They're a lot bigger than me.

MICKEY. There's ways around that.

BOBBY. Like what?

MICKEY. *(Takes roll of nickels out of back pocket.)* Put a roll of nickels in your fist. Makes it hard as a rock. And hit 'em first — when they're not looking. Fight dirty: that's lesson number one.

BOOGER. Guess I'll have another before we go. *(Crosses to bar.)* Give us another round, will you?

DOREEN. You don't look so good, Booger. You have a hard night?

BOOGER. It's hard every night. *(They laugh. He turns, sees BOBBY staring at him.)*

BOBBY. *(picking nose)* How you doin'?

BOOGER. What are you looking at, shitface?

BOBBY. Nothing.

BOOGER. You want a piece of me, is that it? *(Grabs him by his shirt.)* Well, come on, son-of-a-bitch, let's step outside and get it on! *(BOOGER starts dragging BOBBY toward the door. MICKEY stops him and pulls them apart.)*

MICKEY. Hold on! He's just a kid, he don't know any better!

BOOGER. Little son-of-a-bitch was giving me a funny look.

MICKEY. We don't want any trouble.

BOOGER. Who the hell are you, anyway?

MICKEY. I'm Mickey Hollister, and this is Bobby Nobis. Who the hell are you?

BOOGER. I'm Booger McCoy, and I'm paranoid. I been up three days on crystal meth, so don't do nothing to make me suspicious.

MICKEY. Not *the* Booger McCoy who played football for Odessa High?

BOOGER. Yeah, I played a little ball for Odessa.

MICKEY. Why you were all-conference fullback your senior year. I played for Amarillo. You were one stud football player, Booger. Let me buy us a beer.

BOOGER. So you seen me play ball, huh? *(to DOREEN:)* Make them beers on me. Sorry I got a little pissed off there.

MICKEY. That's all right. Been up three days, huh?

BOOGER. Oh, this is nothing. Once I stayed up five days. Started seeing bugs everywhere. Being up three days, I just get to thinking people are plotting behind my back. Why don't you sit down and join us? *(They sit at the table and BOOGER offers his plug of tobacco.)* Have a chew of tobacco?

MICKEY. Sure.

BOOGER. *(offering it to BOBBY)* You?

BOBBY. Little early in the morning for me. *(MICKEY glares at him.)* Don't mind if I do. *(Bites off a mouthful, passes it to POOT.)*

MICKEY. You played pro ball too, didn't you?

BOOGER. A year 'fore I tore up my knee. Been pushing tools ever since. Took rigs to Arabia, Mexico, the North Slope. *(as DOOREEN bring them their beers)* What brings you to Gillette, Hollister?

MICKEY. We're looking for work. Ain't none back in Texas. Heard you say you'd lost a couple of men, Booger? Why don't you sign us on?

BOOGER. You had any experience?

MICKEY. Been roughnecking twenty years now, off and on.

BOOGER. What about your pretty young friend?

MICKEY. Poor Bobby here? No, he ain't had any experience. But his daddy just died and left him without a nickel, and he's got a sick mother. He needs a helping hand.

BOOGER. His hair's mighty long. *(to BOBBY:)* What are you, one of them urban cowboys I been hearing about? Bet you use one of them hot combs, don't you? *(They laugh.)*

MICKEY. Come on, Booger, this is a sure enough good ole boy.

BOOGER. Well, you come to the right place, Hollister. But ain't you getting a little old to roughneck? I don't know if you're still fit enough to do this work.

MICKEY. *(offering hand)* Try me.

BOOGER. I will.

POOT. Lock up! *(They lock hands.)*

MICKEY. Let's make a little eager. If I beat you, then you sign us both on.

BOOGER. Done. *(They look at POOT.)*

POOT. Go for it! *(They begin arm wrestling, BOBBY and POOT urging them on.)* Come on, Booger!

BOBBY. Pull Mickey!

BOOGER. What's your experience, Hollister?

MICKEY. Worked on everything from little spudders to big offshore platforms. Gone from the crown to the ground and back down. Done a little drilling, too.

BOOGER. Job ain't getting any easier, Hollister. It's still the hardest, dirtiest, most dangerous work there is. A man's got to be a jackoff idiot to do it.

BOBBY. Then why do it?

BOOGER. You are an ignorant pissant, aren't you? Remember a few years ago, when they thought we was running out of energy? Looked like the A-rabs had us by the balls. You remember how *that* felt?

MICKEY. Oh, don't get me started on them A-rabs.

BOOGER. You know 'em?

MICKEY. I worked in the Republic of Kuwait. You ask me, we should teach 'em a lesson, right, Bobby?

BOBBY. What?

MICKEY. You know, like I was saying the other day: we ought to teach 'em *lesson number one.*

BOBBY. Oh, yeah, sure! Lesson number one!

MICKEY. *(beginning to strain)* How about it, Booger? I ain't afraid of heights, and I can tote pipe all day long. I got a strong back and a weak mind. I'm the best goddamned roughneck you're ever likely to meet.

POOT. Come on, Booger! Kick his butt! *(BOBBY elbows POOT, who spills his beer down BOOGER'S back. MICKEY pins BOOGER'S fist to the table. BOOGER glares at him, knowing he's been tricked, but decides to let it go.)*

BOOGER. You impress me, Hollister. *(rising)* All right, you boys be here at three-thirty, and Poot'll take you out to the rig. You start at thirteen dollars an hour. Payday's on Monday.

MICKEY. *(shaking his hand)* We really appreciate it, Booger.

BOOGER. Sure.

BOBBY. *(offering his hand)* Everything's gonna be all right, Mr. McCoy. We got a real honcho in the White House now, and he's gonna get tough with them A-rabs.

BOOGER. Amen. *(Puts arm around BOBBY.)* Ain't no energy crisis long as there's good men on the job. This country's got us, and it's got Gillette, and as long as it does the Ayatollah and the rest of them chicken-shiites can just sit in their tents and pull their puddings. *(Grabs at BOBBY'S crotch, laughs.)* Come on, Poot. *(They Exit.)*

MICKEY. Doreen? Give us one of them Slim Jims, will you?

BOBBY. I didn't know you worked in the Republic of Kuwait.

MICKEY. I didn't know you voted for Reagan.

BOBBY. I didn't.

MICKEY. Then you already know lesson number two: always tell the boss what he wants to hear. *(They slap palms.)* Now all we got to do is stay alive until payday.

BOBBY. Jesus, I forgot about that. What are we going to eat?

MICKEY. *(as DOREEN hands him Slim Jim)* This has got to last us three days.

BOBBY. That? I don't want it. It's got nitrates in it.

MICKEY. They're good for you! How do you think a working man keeps going? On nitrates, corn syrup, monosodium glutamate, and all that other good shit. It kept this from spoiling and it'll do the same for you. That's your third lesson. Now eat.

SCENE 2

SCENE: The bar of the Ramada Inn. CATHY and BRENDA, who is very drunk, in a booth. JEETER sits in another booth, wearing a cowboy hat, staring at a glass of beer.

CATHY. Hey, mister? You looking for a good time?

JEETER. Always.

CATHY. Then why don't you come over and buy us a drink?

JEETER. What are you drinkin'?

CATHY. Rusty Nails.

JEETER. What's that?

CATHY. Scotch and Drambuie.

JEETER. You like fancy drinks, don't you?

CATHY. We're fancy women.

JEETER. Well honey, you can put your next round on my tab.

CATHY. *(crossing to him)* What about you?

JEETER. I got to be going home pretty soon.

CATHY. Maybe we can make you a better offer. I'm Cathy, and this is Brenda.

JEETER. How you doin', Brenda?

BRENDA. *(ignoring him)* Fine.

CATHY. You from around here locally?

JEETER. Born and raised.

CATHY. We're from Montana. We're what you might call working girls, if you know what I mean, and we'd like to do a job on you.

JEETER. Why me?

CATHY. Because you look like a nice guy. See, Brenda and me have had some pretty disappointing experiences here. So we decided from now on we're only going to pick nice guys. And you look like the nicest guy here.

JEETER. *(to BRENDA:)* You an Indian?

BRENDA. Why do you ask?

JEETER. You look like one.

BRENDA. You don't like Indians?

JEETER. Did I say that? Hell, no. A lot of people around here don't like Indians, but I got nothing against 'em.

BRENDA. What have they got against them?

JEETER. Well, you know, people think they're strange. They ain't got much to say, and when they do it's something you can't understand. They're good with horses, but they like knives, and sometimes they drink too much and go crazy and try to kill each other.

BRENDA. You think I drink too much?

JEETER. Honey, from what I've seen, everybody in this town drinks too much.

CATHY. Here's our offer. We got a room here at the Ramada Inn. Now you come back there with with us, and we'll both entertain you for the night.

JEETER. Your friend here don't seem to like me too much.

CATHY. She'll warm up to you.

JEETER. I'm not sure I can handle you both.

CATHY. Tell you what: we'll give you a two for the price of one special, tonight only.

JEETER. How much?

CATHY. A hundred dollars.

JEETER. It's a deal.

CATHY. Good. *(rising)* I'm going to the Ladies Room. You better order yourself a plate of mountain oysters. Tonight, you are gonna have the experience of a lifetime. *(She Exits. JEETER crosses to their booth, offers BRENDA a cigarette.)*

BRENDA. My grandfather could talk to animals. *(They stare at each other.)* You don't believe me?

JEETER. If you say so.

BRENDA. He lived way off by himself, in a little shack with a turtle shell nailed over the door. Nobody paid any attention to him. But sometimes I'd bring him a bottle of peach brandy. That's when he told me he could talk to animals. Rabbits, coyotes, prairie dogs. He said he understood antelope the best. They came around at night, when the moon was full, and told him all sorts of shit. Does that sound crazy?

JEETER. Sounds like an Indian.

BRENDA. You mean like an old drunk Indian? Yeah, you're right. That's what he was. But you shoulda heard

that old bastard. He really had it down. He had even me
believing it.

JEETER. What did they tell him?

BRENDA. That there was something wrong with the
world. They told him the moon had lost its way. That this
troubled everyone's sleep and left them confused. *(Stands
unsteadily.)* He said they told him that the world had gotten
so crooked, that to walk straight, you had to lean into the
wind. *(crossing away)* I'm starting to believe him...

JEETER. *(stopping her)* Where you going?

BRENDA. You don't like Indians, do you?

JEETER. I told you, I like 'em.

BRENDA. No you don't. You hate them. And you know
why? Because we're closer to something than you are.

JEETER. Closer? To what?

BRENDA. If you got to ask ... you'll never know.

JEETER. *(bringing her back to table)* You don't know what
the hell you're talking about, do you? Come on, Brenda.
You'd better sit down and cut this shit out before you
make a fool of yourself.

BRENDA. *(breaking away)* My name is Sparkle Ruby
Bird. I belong to the Cree Nation. I went to secretarial
school in Minneapolis, and I can type ninety words a
minute. *(Takes knife out of purse.)* I also carry a knife. *(Presses
button: it clicks open.)* Take your hands off me, white man.
I'm an Indian!

*(He grabs her wrist, forces her to drop the knife. Spins her around
and locks handcuffs on her wrists as CATHY reappears.)*

CATHY. What is this? Take your hands off her—

JEETER. *(shoving her away)* Siddown! *(to BRENDA:)* You have the right to remain silent. You have the right to an attorney.

CATHY. Oh shit...

JEETER. You're both under arrest. For soliciting. *(Shows badge.)* I'm a deputy sheriff of Campbell County. Prostitution's illegal in this town, honey. But we got a place where you can stay for free — the county jail.

SCENE 3

SCENE: A motel room, two weeks later. Two beds, a hotplate, a coffeepot, several cardboard boxes. MICKEY is asleep in his work clothes. BOBBY, who wears clean jeans and a new pair of cowboy boots, is blow-drying his hair.

BOBBY. Mickey? Time to get up.

MICKEY. *(Sits up, puts on hardhat.)* I'm ready. *(but he doesn't move)*

BOBBY. No, Mickey. It's our day off. Time to get up, hit the street, find some girls.

MICKEY. *(Sits up.)* Will you shut that goddamned thing off? *(BOBBY does. He stares at it.)* You do use a hot comb.

BOBBY. Nothing wrong with looking your best, hoss. *(MICKEY flops back onto bed.)* Well, I'm not gonna let this day go to waste. It's the first day off we've had in two weeks. *(Takes out folded square of tinfoil.)* Care to snort some meth?

MICKEY. You're gonna do that shit on your day off?

BOBBY. Come on Mickey, you like your dope.

MICKEY. I got nothing against smoking a little pot, but that shit'll rot your brain.

BOBBY. This is my solution to the energy crisis. *(snorting)* You know, Mickey, this roughnecking is the hardest work I've ever done. But I'm getting the hang of it. Those boys we work with? They're pretty good ole boys. Poot... Chigger ... Booger. I'm even starting to love Booger. *(Notices paper cup full of tobacco juice, picks it up.)* I see he's been here.

MICKEY. Last night, before you come in.

BOBBY. This is the only thing I may never learn to love. *(putting it down carefully)* Filthy habit.

MICKEY. Ain't those new boots?

BOBBY. Yeah, I bought 'em last night.

MICKEY. What did you use for money?

BOBBY. Took some out of the kitty. *(Looks in mirror as MICKEY takes cigar box out from under bed and starts counting money.)* Jesus, look how strong I'm getting. The girls are gonna love this. How about it, Mickey? Think I'm starting to look like a working man?

MICKEY. *(angrily)* You got a long way to go. Now sit down and let me give you a simple lesson in arithmetic. All right, we're making seven hundred a week. But this motel room is costing us fifty a night. And you spent over two hundred dollars on a pair of fancy cowboy boots and a gram of that goddamned crystal meth.

BOBBY. But they're great boots. Elephant hide.

MICKEY. You're spending your coin as fast as you can make it! We came here to work hard, make our pile, and *get out.* I intend to go to Alaska and buy that fishing boat. But if you're not careful, you're gonna get stuck here, like the rest of these fools! *(Throws on denim jacket.)*

BOBBY. Where you going?

MICKEY. Out to get us some breakfast. Then you and me are gonna start looking for a cheaper place to live.

BOBBY. I'll come with you.

MICKEY. No, you stay here and keep an eye on our things. I don't like the look of some of the characters I've seen around this motel.

BOBBY. But this was supposed to be my day off. I was gonna have some fun.

MICKEY. *(at door)* Get in some practice on that guitar. You need it. *(Exits.)*

BOBBY. Total bullshit.

(He puts on a Stetson, looks at himself in mirror. Then he picks up his guitar and sits on bed, playing softly. A KNOCK. He goes to the door.)

BOBBY. Who is it?

JODY. *(through door)* Could you open the door please? *(He does.)* Hey, cowboy. Think you could let me in?

BOBBY. Sure.

(JODY Enters, offers her hand. She wears a leather jacket, jeans and boots.)

JODY. I'm Jody.

BOBBY. Bobby.

JODY. I'm staying right next door.

BOBBY. What do you need?

JODY. Company. I thought maybe you and me could get to know each other a little better.

BOBBY. Is something the matter?

JODY. I had a fight with my ole man, that's all. He's a real bad dude. Do you think I could just sit here for a minute until I got my shit together?

BOBBY. Stay as long as you like.

JODY. *(looking toward the door)* He'll come looking for me.

BOBBY. He's not gonna find you here. And if he does, I can take care of him. Here, why don't you put this Space Blanket around you, and I'll get you a cup of coffee. *(He puts Space Blanket around her shoulders, crosses to hotplate.)*

JODY. You cowboys really know how to treat the girls, don't you?

BOBBY. What did you fight about?

JODY. He just lost another job. Came home drunk and informed me it was time for *me* to go to work. Said he know somebody who could get me a job as a mud wrestler.

BOBBY. *(starting toward door)* Maybe I better go teach him a lesson.

JODY. Go on, then! And when you do, tell him I'm sick and tired of hopping on his motorcycle and roaring off to another state every time I turn around.

BOBBY. *(at door)* He's got a motorcycle?

JODY. Oh yeah, this big ole Harley hog. He loves it more than he loves me. This dude in Salt Lake City just looked at it the wrong way and Sonny put him in the hospital.

BOBBY. *(locking door)* How'd you meet this guy?

JODY. Answered a letter in *Rolling Stone* saying he was, you know, a convict, and he was looking for some nice girl to write him. So we got this little correspondence going, and when he got out of Soledad he just showed up one day on his bike, and by that time I was good and ready to get out of Tucson.

BOBBY. *(bringing her a cup of coffee)* Well, I'd say a girl who falls in love with a convict is deeply insecure. She's looking for someone she can feel superior to.

JODY. *(suspiciously)* That's the same bullshit the psychiatrist gave me. Where'd you hear it?

BOBBY. I had a little college.

JODY. I thought you were a *cowboy.*

BOBBY. Well, I've always been a cowboy at heart.

JODY. *(scornfully)* I mean I thought you were a *real* cowboy, who lived off in the mountains someplace, and only came down to ride in the rodeo. *(starting toward door)* I'll never meet a really cool guy. I'll be a loser forever—

BOBBY. Hold on! You don't have to go yet. I'm trying to help you. *(Tries to stop her, spills coffee on shirt.)* Shit!

JODY. Sorry.

BOBBY. I just bought this shirt.

JODY. *(Hesitates.)* You got another one?

BOBBY. Yeah, but it's not ironed.

JODY. I'll do it for you. You were gonna let me stay here, it's the least I can do. Where's your iron?

BOBBY. In that box.

JODY. Get your shirt. I'll do it right here on the bed. *(She plugs in iron, spreads towel on bed.)*

BOBBY. *(getting shirt)* Do your parents know where you are?

JODY. They don't care. Anyway, they're divorced. My father ran off and left me with my mother, who is totally shitty. She comes on to all my boyfriends. *(as he give her shirt)* Take that one off.

BOBBY. Why?

JODY. It's got coffee all over it. *(when he hesitates)* What's the matter, don't you think I've ever seen a dude with his shirt off before? *(ironing, as he removes shirt)* I tried to run off once, but she hired a cop to bring me back. Then one day I bought a copy of *Rolling Stone* and I saw Sonny's letter — "Bro in prison doing one to five seeks Aryan honey interested in hitting the road" — and I thought maybe he'd take me so far away she'd never find me. We lived in six different states before we came here. Boy, I'm telling you, this town can really do a number on your head.

BOBBY. It's not place for a nice girl like you.

JODY. *(smiling)* What about you? You're a college boy. How'd you end up in Gillette?

BOBBY. My degree's in Radio-Television. The only job I could get in Amarillo was selling computer software for Montgomery Ward's. I couldn't stand it, so I quit and started hitchhiking out to Los Angeles. Mickey picked me up and said if we came here, we could make big coin.

JODY. So you're here for the money, just like everybody else.

BOBBY. Is something wrong with that?

JODY. That's all my mother cares about. She's always saying, find yourself a rich guy with lots of money.

BOBBY. *(picking up guitar)* Well, I'm not here just for the money. I'm looking for something better.

JODY. What's that?

BOBBY. Experience. *(playing guitar softly)* I been fooling around with this guitar for years, but I've never written any songs. Nothing to say, I guess. One day at work I was watching Merle Haggard on this big pile of television sets. And I thought: Merle Haggard didn't become an artist by selling computer software for Montgomery Ward. He went out and got experience in his youth. And so many things have happened to me since I came here. Why, for three days Mickey and I lived on a Slim Jim. I could never have had that experience if I'd stayed in Amarillo.

JODY. *(laughs)* You know, Bobby, I've never met anyone like you before. But I like you.

BOBBY. That's what I'm here for: to see this life, learn everything about it, and write songs.

JODY. *(appreciatively)* All right.

BOBBY. 'Course it'd be easier if I had a girl to inspire me. But the girls in this town take one look at me, and all they see is that I ain't got big coin.

JODY. I always fall for the guy — who he is, not what he's got in his pocket.

BOBBY. That's how it should be.

JODY. But he's got to be able to take care of himself. *(standing, holding up shirt to his body)* How's it look?

BOBBY. Fine.

JODY. You were really gonna do it, weren't you?

BOBBY. What?

JODY. Fight my ole man.

BOBBY. If I had to.

JODY. You'll find a girl, Bobby.

BOBBY. You think so?

JODY. It won't take you long.

BOBBY. *(kissing her)* Maybe I just did.

JODY. Bobby, you shouldn't be doing this.

BOBBY. Jody, you've got to get away from this guy. Why don't you let me help you?

JODY. You're taking a big chance, Bobby.

BOBBY. I like taking chances.

(He kisses her again, they fall onto the bed. Someone POUNDS on the door. BOBBY jumps to his feet.)

BOBBY. I knew it.

SONNY. *(through door)* Jody?

JODY. Don't open that door.

BOBBY. Don't worry.

SONNY. *(pounding)* I know you're in there, Jody. Open this goddamned door!

BOBBY. *(shouting)* Now listen! Your ole lady doesn't want to see you right now, and there's nothing you can do about it. So why don't you just take a hike before I come out there and stomp the shit out of you? *(Silence. He looks at JODY.)* Is he gone?

JODY. I hope so.

(SONNY'S fist smashes through the wall beside the door.)

BOBBY. *Oh shit!*

(SONNY enlarges the hole with more blows, reaches through, unlocks the door and Enters. He has long hair and conspicuous tattoos.)

SONNY. A cowboy. She's got a thing for cowboys, don't you, Jody? *(to BOBBY:)* You hit on her?

BOBBY. Absolutely nothing happened.

SONNY. *(to JODY:)* He hit on you? *(She avoids his eye.)* I thought so. *(moving around room)* You got a lot of shit here. You got a hotplate ... tire tools. *(Picks up cardboard box.)* What's this?

BOBBY. My buddy's record collection, leave it alone!

SONNY. *(turning toward him)* You're not afraid of me, are you, cowboy?

BOBBY. You'd better go.

SONNY. You screwed up this time, cowboy. I can't have any loose brag going around about how you hit on my ole lady and got away with it, can I?

BOBBY. What do you think you're gonna do about it?

SONNY. What am I gonna do?

BOBBY. Yeah.

SONNY. Nail your ass to the floor. *(picking up hammer from toolbox)* With this.

BOBBY. You just try it. *(when SONNY starts toward him)* All right, all right. Where do you want me to sit?

SONNY. Right there. *(BOBBY sits and SONNY starts nailing the seat of his pants to the floor with careful blows, enjoying his work.)*

BOBBY. Jody, tell him nothing happened.

JODY. You're on your own now, Bobby. I hate to see a dude shoot his mouth off when he can't back it up.

BOBBY. You know why she's doing this, don't you? She's trying to make you jealous. I understand this now. She probably loves you very much and she wants you to show her that you love her too. But you're probably not very good at expressing your feelings.

SONNY. You found yourself a real interesting guy this time, Jody.

BOBBY. This wouldn't even be happening, if you knew how to express your feelings.

SONNY. This is how I express my feelings. *(Finishes, rises.)* Let's see what else you got here. *(looking around)* A guitar ... a radio. *(Picks up cigar box full of money.)*

BOBBY. Hey!

SONNY. *(opening it)* Why, there must be four or five hundred dollars here. *(putting money in pocket)* Tell you what: you can keep the record collection. *(picking up guitar and hotplate)* But you tried to hit on my ole lady, cowboy, and I've got to have my satisfaction. *(to JODY:)* I'm loading this shit on my scoot, then we're getting out of here. *(to BOBBY:)* Stay put: I'll be right back.

(He Exits. We hear the sound of a diesel AIR HORN as a TRAIN pulls out of the nearby railroad yards.)

BOBBY. Well, Jody, this is real depressing.

JODY. You deserve it, Bobby. You made a fool of yourself all the way.

BOBBY. Jody, this guy is dangerous.

JODY. He's got a lot of problems, Bobby. See, he's just a prospect — he's not affiliated with a club yet, and he's trying to find one that'll have him.

BOBBY. You've got to get rid of him.

JODY. Someday I might need him. *(Drops to floor beside him.)* The big shitstorm's coming down, Bobby. It's coming soon.

BOBBY. The big shitstorm?

JODY. Nuclear war. Sonny's ready for it. He's got a gun, and he's got a ton of canned goods buried up in the Big Horn National Forest. He says we'll go up there when it happens, and kill a deer and jerk the meat. We'll survive.

BOBBY. But it might not happen. If everybody gets together and stops it...

JODY. Everybody *wants* it to happen, Bobby. Secretly. It means they're never gonna get old — so they can go on getting all they can right now. But ever since I was a little girl I've known that someday there's gonna be this flash of light... and everything's gonna just *stop. (Stares at him for a moment with terror in her eyes, then goes on.)* And when it does, I'm going to be with a lower-class dude. Because then money won't mean anything, just strength. And I'm sorry, Bobby, but you just haven't got it.

(SONNY Reenters.)

SONNY. All right, baby. *(She Exits. SONNY nails BOB-BY'S shirtsleeves to the floor so that he is lying flat on his back.)* You're not gonna beef to the cops about this, are you, cowboy?

BOBBY. What have you got against cowboys?

SONNY. I don't like nostalgia. It's over, but you guys don't know it yet.

(Sound of diesel AIR HORN.)

SONNY. You hear that coal train?

BOBBY. Yeah.

SONNY. I loaded them trains out at the Thunder Basin strip mine. They ship a thousand tons of coal out of here every day. That's what this country's all about now. Used to be beef. Now it's coal and oil. But you guys ain't caught on to that yet. You still want to ride and rope. Bet you just love the smell of horse shit, don't you?

BOBBY. Sure.

SONNY. Smell I like best is gasoline. My daddy had a filling station in Corvallis. We used to smell gasoline. Used to get high on it. *(finishing, rising)* The thing I hate most about you is, you're all alike. And I hate you. I hate your boots. And your hats. And your fucking Skoal. *(Picks up BOOGER'S cup of tobacco juice.)*

BOBBY. I'm not really a cowboy.

SONNY. You don't ride the lone prairie? Or do the Cotton-Eyed Joe?

BOBBY. Actually, I sell computer software for Montgomery Ward.

SONNY. *(holding cup under BOBBY'S nose)* Drink it.

BOBBY. What?

SONNY. *Drink it!* Or do I have to beat the dogshit out of you? *(BOBBY drinks it, goes into a fit of coughing.)* Now you're a cowboy. *(at door)* Don't even think about going to the cops. There's more than one dead body left this town under a load of coal. Those trains go down to a power plant in Texas and they dump that coal into a big furnace. Two thousand degrees. You fuck with me, cowboy, and I'll send you back down to Texas to keep the lights burning.

(He Exits. Sound of MOTORCYCLE leaving as BOBBY coughs. Then MICKEY reappears in the doorway.)

MICKEY. Explain this! Where's my radio? My hotplate? The kitty? What in the hell has happened here?

BOBBY. We got ripped off.

MICKEY. Couldn't even leave you alone for five minutes, could I? *(Looks closer.)* Hell, boy, you're nailed to the floor. I knowed you were stupid, but this time you outdone yourself! *(getting hammer, starting to pry up nails)* Who was it?

BOBBY. This biker. He busted right through the door looking for his girl, and when he found her he was so pissed off he took all our coin.

MICKEY. What was she doing here?

BOBBY. I let her in.

MICKEY. Thought you were gonna get laid, didn't you?

BOBBY. No, I was just trying to help her. Mickey, I'm in love! She doesn't care about that guy. She needs somebody like me.

MICKEY. She left with him, didn't she?

BOBBY. That's why we got to catch 'em, Mickey. We've got to help that girl!

MICKEY. *(pulling him to his feet)* We got to catch 'em, all right. I want my shit back. Something you got to learn about boom towns, son. Don't trust nobody. Especially don't trust the women. They're here for one reason, and that's to get what they can, same as you.

BOBBY. I think I'm gonna be sick...

MICKEY. You oughta be.

BOBBY. I suppose there's a lesson in this.

MICKEY. Yeah, there's a lesson: don't let your dingus do your thinking for you. Now come on, let's go!

SCENE 4

SCENE: The Campbell County Jail. BRENDA and CATHY scrubbing floors under the glare of a single incandescent light.

CATHY. You know, Brenda, I think there's something seriously wrong with men. They're not even logical. All they think about is sex, right?

BRENDA. Right.

CATHY. Then why did they make it *illegal?*

BRENDA. Pass me that bucket, will you?

CATHY. I'm just trying to find some meaning in this, that's all. *(lighting cigarette)* That time you were in jail before...

BRENDA. Fargo, North Dakota.

CATHY. Was it this bad?

BRENDA. It was worse.

CATHY. I don't see how it could be much worse than this. This place has got to be the cockroach capital of the world. I don't care for the food much, either. First thing I'm gonna do when I get out is go to Burger King. *(pause)* You ever miss men?

BRENDA. Never. *(pause)*

CATHY. Brenda? Did you ever think you might have a chip on your shoulder?

BRENDA. Why? Because I'm an Indian?

CATHY. No, because you're a hooker. Sometimes it seems like you hate men or something.

BRENDA. I don't hate 'em. I've just decided to do without 'em.

CATHY. Maybe we're doing this all wrong.

BRENDA. How do you mean?

CATHY. Trying to go independent.

BRENDA. I told you: I'm not splitting my score with anybody. I'm doing this for myself.

CATHY. Yeah, but my manager was a bail bondsman. He could have had us out of here in five minutes.

BRENDA. We don't need those shitbirds. That's where most girls go wrong, they split their money with a pimp. We work for ourselves, we can make enough money to buy some property. Then we can rent it out and never have to work again.

CATHY. Yeah, but Brenda? The next time you're talking to a guy and you think he might be a cop?

BRENDA. Yeah?

CATHY. Just don't pull a knife on him, all right?

BRENDA. All right, I'm sorry. *(pause)* We just came to the wrong town, that's all. When we get out of here, we'll go to Rock Springs. They're building a pipeline there.

CATHY. If we ever *do* get out. Oh god, I hate this place.

BRENDA. I kind of like it. The first week's always the worst. You think you've got to have a drink or die. But finally it all goes away. You don't care if they ever let you out. You do laundry and scrub the floors. You remember things. Then comes the day they let you out. Your clothes feel funny. You put on lipstick. Your perfume smells so strong it makes you sick. I walked down North Pacific Avenue and ate a sugar doughnut. It was the best thing I ever ate in my life. You take a drink, and you're disappointed it doesn't taste better. You think, I'm gonna do fine. You feel strong. You won't get angry this time, you won't get drunk. It's enough to be able to come and go. But the best things are the things no one notices. The sky. The clouds. The door you can walk out any time you please. That's when I decided I was gonna go independent. And we're gonna do it, Cathy. We're gonna make it work. We just came to the wrong town, that's all.

CATHY. I'll never get the smell of Lysol out of my hair...

BRENDA. *(putting her arm around her)* Cheer up, kid: only fourteen more days to go.

SCENE 5

SCENE: An oil rig south of Gillette. Steel girders silhouetted against a blue sky, the CHUGGING of diesel engines. POOT and CHIGGER, a roughneck with long hair and a beard, are cleaning tools when MICKEY and BOBBY Enter.

CHIGGER. Booger's been looking for you guys.

BOBBY. We'd better go see what he wants.

MICKEY. Take it easy. *(looking at watch)* We don't have to go to work for two more minutes yet. How was *your* day off, Poot?

POOT. Shitty.

MICKEY. Couldn't have been any shittier than ours. We spent the whole day looking for the son-of-a-bitch who stole everything we owned.

POOT. *(drinking from a halfpint of bourbon)* Be glad you ain't me. I spent my day drinking at the Boot Hill Bar. Gave 'em a nine hundred dollar paycheck to cash and told 'em to run me a tab. That's the last thing I remember. Went back this morning for my change, and they told me I owed *them* three hundred forty-four dollars and forty-eight cents.

MICKEY. That *is* pretty shitty.

POOT. I had a thousand dollars worth of fun, and I can't even remember it.

MICKEY. Well, there's once consolation in touching bottom, Poot. You know things can't get any worse.

(BOOGER Enters.)

BOOGER. There you are.

MICKEY. What do you need, Booger?

BOOGER. All right, everybody, listen up. I got some good news and some bad news. Well's come in, so as soon as we lay casing, we'll be tearing down the rig and moving on. Lone Star Drilling Company says we don't need but three men for that. Nobis, I'm gonna have to lay you off.

BOBBY. *(sitting)* Oh shit...

BOOGER. Here's the good news. I just scored some primo crystal meth. Should make the job go a lot faster for those that stay.

MICKEY. Bullshit! *(to the others:)* It's gonna be a hell of a job for three men to tear down this rig. You see what he's doing, don't you? He's trying to get three men to do the work of four. And he figures he's gonna do it by giving you drugs.

CHIGGER. If I got to work harder, I want drugs.

MICKEY. You would. *(to BOOGER:)* That's why you have so many accidents on this rig, Booger. You're turning your men into a bunch of goddamned drooling meth freaks!

BOOGER. Hollister, do yu want to keep your job?

MICKEY. I don't work unless Bobby works!

BOOGER. Just step over here, Hollister.

MICKEY. *(rolling up his sleeves)* Anywhere you want, Booger.

BOOGER. None of that shit. Just step over here and have a word with me. *(to others:)* You boys get in a circle and shine your tools. *(They step out of earshot of the others.)* Think you're a real swinging dick, don't you, Hollister? Now you listen and listen good. Lone Star's spudding in another well next week. They're looking for another toolpusher, and I told 'em yu got the know-how. You keep your mouth shut, and I'll see you get to boss that rig.

MICKEY. What about Bobby?

BOOGER. He could work a thousand years and he'd still be a weevil. What do you say, Hollister? Ain't no future in roughnecking.

MICKEY. I don't think I want your job, Booger. I'm too smart to spend the rest of my life kissing some company's ass. I intend to be a lot more than just a toolpusher someday.

BOOGER. *(hurt)* I ain't smart enough to be a high roller. I know that. I work for other people. But I pull down forty thou a year pushing tools. I got a home in Odessa, a bass boat, and once a year I can take the wife and kids to Six Flags. It ain't a bad life. But you, Hollister, you got nothing to show for your years.

MICKEY. Maybe not, but I'm gonna make a big score someday, Booger — and I'm gonna do it my own way!

BOOGER. I don't see you making no big score. I see you ending up a sad ole fool on a barstool somewhere, asking people to buy you drinks so you can tell them the story of your life. Now do you want the job or not?

MICKEY. *(loud enough for the other to hear)* I told you: I don't work unless Bobby works! And you guys shouldn't either!

BOOGER. *(to the others:)* You heard what he said. All right, Hollister. You're fired. And now I'm gonna show you something. Your boy may be stupid, but he ain't as stupid as you. Come over here, Nobis. *(when BOBBY crosses to them)* Hollister don't want to work. How about you? You ain't much, but I can keep one man.

BOBBY. *(grinning at MICKEY)* Same goes for me.

BOOGER. If that's the way you want it. But I'll tell you something, Hollister: your buddy ain't worth it. He don't love the job.

BOBBY. I try, Booger.

BOOGER. The hell you do. You don't see what we're doing here is important. America needs energy — and if we don't get it, your children are going to grow up reading the Koran and worshipping the Ayatollah Khomeini! *(stuffing bills in MICKEY'S shirt pocket)* But you're a good man, Hollister, and I hate to see you do this to yourself. Now get the hell off my rig! *(to the others: as he goes)* Come on, girls, we got work to do! *(Everyone Exits but POOT.)*

BOBBY. Jesus, Mickey, what are we gonna do now?

MICKEY. Get drunk. Sometimes it's the only thing to do. *(to POOT:)* Poot, I'll give you twenty dollars for that bottle. You need the money, don't you?

POOT. Sure.

MICKEY. Then don't think about it, just give it to me. *(He gives POOT BOOGER'S money, POOT gives him the bottle.)*

POOT. Well, I be dog. *(Exits.)*

MICKEY. *(arm around BOBBY)* Let's get in the ole Ford and go for a drive. We need some answers, son — and I think we're gonna find 'em somewhere out there on that prairie.

SCENE 6

SCENE: *Rig sillhouette flies up and out of sight to reveal the open prairie. In the foreground, three strands of fence wire and a cow skull. In the remote distance, toylike oil rigs. SUN-*

LIGHT pours down out of the open sky. MICKEY approaches the fence, drinking from the halfpint of bourbon.

MICKEY. Well there she is, son! The wide open spaces! Nothing out there but miles and miles of miles and miles!

BOBBY. Yeah, there's only one problem: it all belongs to somebody else.

MICKEY. Let's see if we can't do something about that. *(Produces a pair of wire cutters, clips fence wire.)* After you.

BOBBY. Hey, Mickey, I don't know if this is such a good idea—

MICKEY. *(stepping through)* Why, there ain't a cop for fifty miles. Step on out here, where you can breathe for a change. *(BOBBY does.)* Ain't that better? Now look out there. What do you see?

BOBBY. Nothing.

MICKEY. That's the point, son.

BOBBY. It's beautiful, I got to admit it.

MICKEY. Beautiful? It's more than that. It's freedom itself. Why you can blow your top out here, and nobody cares. *(He yells at the top of his lungs, falls over on the ground as the echoes die away.)*

BOBBY. What do you think you're doing?

MICKEY. I'm studying the sky. The western sky is a beautiful shade of blue like you see nowhere else. Get on down here and get an eyeful. *(BOBBY sits next to him.)*

BOBBY. Mickey? Why'd you give up that job?

MICKEY. I don't want to be a goddamned toolpusher! You take a job like that, you give up your freedom. My

future is in Alaska, not in working for the Lone Star Drilling Company — and besides, it was worth it just to see the look on Booger's face.

BOBBY. *(getting up)* Well I've had enough. I'm leaving.

MICKEY. What do you mean?

BOBBY. I'm going back to Amarillo.

MICKEY. *(stopping him)* You're not gonna let a little misfortune get you down, are you?

BOBBY. A little misfortune! Look, if I'm gonna starve to death, I'd rather do it back in Amarillo! And if you had any sense, you'd come with me.

MICKEY. I won't let you go. You ain't learned enough yet! You run on back to the suburbs now, and you'll never amount to shit!

BOBBY. Well I'm going!

MICKEY. *(shoving him through gap in fence)* Go on, then! Run on out on me, if that's what you want! Run on back to Texas and work for Monkey Ward's! But I'm staying! *(turning away)* You only get a boom like this every twenty years or so, and I ain't getting any younger. I missed the North Slope. When guys like Booger were making their pile, I was dodging Vietcong bullets. But I'm not gonna miss Gillette! It's my last chance to make my pile, and I'm not leaving until I do...

BOBBY. *(stepping back through fence)* All right, Mickey. I'll stick with you ... for a while.

MICKEY. *(arm around him)* I knew you wouldn't disappoint me son. You're my friend, and sometimes friendship's all a working man's got. *(They slap palms.)*

BOBBY. But what are we gonna do for money? We're

just as broke as the day we got here.

MICKEY. *(Pulls money out of sock.)* Well, I got a couple a hundred bills stashed away. That should see us through.

BOBBY. It ain't gonna last long in that town.

MICKEY. *(Rises.)* Maybe we don't have to back to that town. I been thinking. Problem with that town is, you got to spend all your coin just keeping a roof over your head.

BOBBY. Yeah?

MICKEY. Well, who says we got to have a roof? Why can't we just live right here?

BOBBY. But this is somebody's property!

MICKEY. He's only got about a million acres. Don't you think he can spare us some room? We'll have solar heat and nature's own air-conditioning! What do you say, son? Why go back to that town, where you got to live like a rat in a cage, when we can set up housekeeping right here?

BOBBY. Mickey, you are a truly original thinker. I never would have thought of it, but there's no reason why we can't live out here for nothing!

MICKEY. Then let this be another lesson to you: if you don't like the game, don't play by their rules!

BOBBY. *(slapping his palm)* Yeah! *(Sits.)* But there's still one thing missing.

MICKEY. What?

BOBBY. Girls.

MICKEY. I been thinking about that too. True, we're getting nowhere with the girls in Gillette. Thing we got to do is find some girls who are so far down that even we look good to 'em. And I think I know where to look.

BOBBY. Where?

MICKEY. Jail.

BOBBY. We've got to go to *jail?*

MICKEY. 'Course not. All we got to do is hang around *outside* the local jail and hit on the first two ladies who come out.

BOBBY. *(thinking)* There must be girls in that hail who are starved for affection. Girls who haven't had their hands on a man in months ... *(He stands, yells, throws his hat in the air.)* Mickey, I got to hand it to you. you just may have come up with a great idea!

MICKEY. Trust me, son. I may have gotten us into this — but I can promise you I'm gonna get us out.

(They slap palms. BLACKOUT.)

ACT II
SCENE 1

SCENE: *The prairie where we last saw BOBBY and MICKEY,*
two weeks later. Under the open sky there a sofa which folds
out into a bed, a large easy chair, a standing lamp, a tele-
vision set, a record player with a speaker on a long cord, a
refrigerator, four car batteries, and a Hibachi which sends
up a curl of smoke. MICKEY and BOBBY Enter, start
spreading tablecloth on ground.

BOBBY. Mickey, you're a genius! And they're a lot
better looking than I thought they'd be! You take the old
one and I'll take the young one.

MICKEY. What if the young one's got other ideas?

BOBBY. How could she go for an old dog like you?

MICKEY. I think we should let them decide.

BOBBY. Well I don't.

(BRENDA and CATHY Enter.)

MICKEY. Welcome to our happy home!

BRENDA. Where?

MICKEY. You're looking at it.

BRENDA. All I see is some old furniture somebody
dumped out here in the middle of nowhere.

MICKEY. Now don't go knocking our furniture: it's the

46

finest the Salvation Army's got to offer.

CATHY. But where's your house?

BOBBY. I don't think we ever mentioned a house. And you've got to admit, the view is spectacular.

CATHY. *(to BRENDA:)* Maybe we should go.

MICKEY. Not until you've experienced our hospitality. See what's in the icebox, will you, Bobby?

BOBBY. *(opening icebox door)* My, oh my. Four big sirloin steaks.

MICKEY. The Hibachi's all fired up. Think you could drop 'em on the grill?

BOBBY. Can do. *(Puts steaks on grill.)*

MICKEY. *(turning on television)* And while you're waiting, you ladies can make yourselves comfortable and watch some TV.

CATHY. Where do you get your electricity from?

BOBBY. Four big Delco batteries.

MICKEY. Reception's not so hot, but we're thinking about getting a satellite dish from Montgomery Ward's. Bobby's got connections. As you can see, we're not ordinary men.

BRENDA. No, I can see that.

MICKEY. *(producing a bottle)* Could I offer you ladies a drink? It's happy hour, and I just happen to have a bottle of sippin' whiskey here. Austin Nichols Wild Turkey — only the best there is.

BRENDA. Look, we're not ladies. We're hookers.

CATHY. And we just got out of jail.

MICKEY. I don't mind. *(to BOBBY:)* Do you mind?

BOBBY. Doesn't bother me.

MICKEY. As a matter of fact, I've always wanted to meet

a hooker so I could tell her how much I admire the profession. You ladies practice the oldest art in the world — the art of love — and what could be wrong with that?

CATHY. He's *cool.*

BRENDA. Well, we're a little short of money, and we were thinking if you boys were looking for a good time tonight—

MICKEY. You mean *sex?*

BRENDA. Yeah.

MICKEY. *(shaking his head)* No, no, no. First of all, no money's going to change hands tonight. That would just spoil it. It may surprise you, but sex isn't all that important to me anyway. How about you, Bobby?

BOBBY. It's way down on my list.

MICKEY. You see, Bobby and me have been out here without women for so long we just want to...

BOBBY. Worship you, you might say.

MICKEY. Treat you like the beautiful creatures you are. As we see it, you ladies have been treated wrongly by society. So we're gonna make it up to you. We offer you good food, drinks, some pleasant conversation. If things go beyond that, fine...

BOBBY. But you're under no obligation. And you will find us perfect gentlemen.

MICKEY. Is that clear?

BRENDA. *(disappointed)* I guess so.

MICKEY. Then all you ladies have to do is tell us how you'd like your steaks.

BRENDA. *(Thinks; then.)* Oh, what the hell. Make mine rare.

CATHY. Well done.

MICKEY. Fine. Then let's drop all this heavy conversation and eat. But first, we'll smoke a nice fat joint and watch the sun go down. Watching the sun go down is the big entertainment around here. When it's real good, we applaud. *(The girls relax, sit on couch. MICKEY pours them drinks. BOBBY is stuck with the cooking.)*

BOBBY. Where are you ladies from?

CATHY. We met each other in Billings. Heard about Gillette and thought we'd come here and try freelancing for a while. Everybody said it was the place to go. Boy, were they ever wrong.

BRENDA. You got a real low class of customer here. Somebody stold my purse, somebody gave her a black eye.

CATHY. After this, I'm going into telephone sex.

BRENDA. Then to top it off, we got busted and did thirty days.

CATHY. They made us do tons of laundry and scrub floors.

BRENDA. We were trying to save enough money to buy a condo in Vail, but we didn't make a nickel.

MICKEY. Doesn't sound like jail's changed much.

BRENDA. You been in jail? What for?

MICKEY. Grand Theft Auto. I jump-started a Ford Fairlaine with a paperclip and drove to Waco to see a girl. Oh, I never done anything to hurt anyone — just youthful hell-raising.

CATHY. Well, I feel sorry for you.

MICKEY. Don't. I learned something from the experience. I think you should learn something from everything you undergo: if you don't, your life's just a trip to nowhere.

CATHY. *(crossing to MICKEY)* What'd you learn?

MICKEY. That it all comes down to what you make of it, just like everything else. There was a poem scratched on the wall of my cell I've never forgotten. It goes like this:

Two men looked at the world through prison bars
One saw mud — but the other saw stars.

CATHY. *(fascinated with MICKEY)* That's *beautiful.*

BRENDA. Sounds like a lot of bullshit, if you ask me.

CATHY. Know what your problem is, Brenda? You don't trust people enough. You think everybody's out to mess you over. *(to MICKEY:)* I think you're a pretty cool guy.

BRENDA. Well, I say he's trying to get something for nothing, and that's why he's handing us all this bullshit.

MICKEY. You and me have got to have a serious talk. *(lighting a joint and passing it around)* Can't you get it through your head that I respect you?

BRENDA. Why should you?

MICKEY. For one thing, you already know what it takes most women a lifetime to learn — how to be your own boss.

BRENDA. *(grudgingly)* Yeah, that's so. I go where I want and I say what I please. Nobody tells me what to do.

MICKEY. Society may condemn you, but conventional morality aside, you're a hell of a good business-woman.

CATHY. *(nodding)* That's why I became a hooker. One day I realized I was sitting on top of the greatest little commodity in the world. You got it, you sell it, you still got it.

MICKEY. And you're not a hypocrite. You take those women in Gillette. Oh, they'll let you make love to them, but first you've got to buy 'em food and clothes and dope, all sorts of shit. Oh, they're selling it. They're just not out front about it, like you. And you're probably very good at what you do, while most of them ain't.

BRENDA. *(bitterly)* But most guys don't appreciate that. They just want you to lie there, moaning and groaning and telling them how good *they* are. They don't care about quality. Paying for it's the important thing.

MICKEY. That's what's wrong with America today. People worship the almighty coin, instead of respecting someone for what they do well. In the days of ancient Greece and Rome, women who practiced the art of love were celebrities. They had great respect.

BRENDA. *(smiling, starting to enjoy MICKEY)* You don't really believe all these things you're saying, do you?

MICKEY. Well ... I do and I don't.

BRENDA. That's all right. You're making the effort. *(BOBBY has taken steaks off grill and put them on paper plates. By now, the sun is setting.)*

BOBBY. Dinner is served! *(Everyone sits on ground and starts eating.)* How is it?

CATHY. Super good.

BRENDA. I'll say one thing for jail: when you get out, everything's great for a while — even your bullshit. Food tastes great, the world looks great...

CATHY. I'll say. Just look at that sunset.

BRENDA. Everything in glorious technicolor.

BOBBY. This is pretty good pot ... *(For another moment they stare at the sunset, stoned. Then MICKEY comes to his feet and starts applauding.)*

MICKEY. Bravo, god! Primo! *(Everyone applauds.)* Now — what say we listen to my Roy Orbison records?

BOBBY. Hey, Mickey? Let's not listen to those records, all right? *(to girls:)* That's what he does every time he gets stoned: listens to Roy Orbison and has a religious experience.

MICKEY. Am I to understand ... would I be boring you ladies if I...

CATHY. *(to BRENDA:)* Who's Roy Orbison?

MICKEY. You never heard of him?

BRENDA. He was before your time.

MICKEY. *(taking CATHY'S arm and leading her to record player)* He's a great artist. Come on, get your steak and sit right here by the speaker so you can get the full effect.

BOBBY. But you'd better listen close, 'cause he always talks right through it.

MICKEY. *(taking record out of cardboard box)* I've carried these records with me everywhere for twenty years, and why not? They're worth their weight in gold. *(With dignity, he puts on record, and we hear Roy Orbison singing *It's Over.)*

BRENDA. That's nice.

MICKEY. *(unable to contain himself)* Like a cold wind blowing across the Texas panhandle. Like a blue norther. That's the sound of Texas in my youth. And Roy was there.

BOBBY. *(to CATHY:)* See what I mean?

---

* Cautionary Note: Permission to produce this play does *not* include permission to use this music in performance.

MICKEY. He was born in Wink. I met him one night in Lubbock. Shook his hand. He was wearing those shades like he always does. Nobody's ever seen the look in his eyes but it's all there in his voice. Lonliness, that's what you're hearing. Am I wrong? *(Eyes closed, as music builds.)* Cold motel rooms where you got laid for the first time. High school football games where you were a hero. The man had a voice that spanned three octaves. And he could make it drip blood when he wanted. So powerful... so mysterious ... and above all, *so lonely (singing along with record) It's over! It's over! (Everyone is laughing at him. He glares at BOBBY.)* What's so goddamned funny?

BOBBY. He does this every time.

MICKEY. Oh *all right. (He rips needle off record player.)*

BRENDA. Mickey...

MICKEY. It's my *youth ... (turning to BOBBY)* You know, there's a lot of things you do that I don't like.

BOBBY. Oh come on! I wasn't the only one laughing at you.

MICKEY. No, but you could show a little more consideration for other people's feelings.

BRENDA. They sound like old married folk, don't they?

MICKEY. *(pulling BOBBY away)* Let's not air our problems in front of these ladies. *(bitterly)* I just want to say that when people live this closely, all sorts of frictions develop. And you *could* show a little more consideration for my feelings.

BOBBY. What about my feelings? I'm sick of those records, if you want to know the truth. You've only made me listen to 'em about a thousand times. You've got no idea what it's like to live with him!

MICKEY. That's enough out of you!

BOBBY. You've always got to have things *your* way. Do this, do that. I mean, I'd love to go into town sometime and get away from you, but oh no, you won't let me have the keys to the car!

MICKEY. When you're man enough, you can come take 'em!

BOBBY. See what I mean? What makes you think you got the right to boss me around all the time? I'm sorry, Mickey, but sometimes you act like this is your house and I'm your goddamned wife or something!

MICKEY. One more word out of you — *(MICKEY breaks off, goes and sits in chair in front of television set. Silence.)*

BRENDA. You boys have just got a touch of cabin fever, that's all.

CATHY. I don't know, Brenda. Seems like in every relationship, somebody's got to dominate the other person.

BRENDA. Do they?

CATHY. Sure, you know, like when you try to come on like my big sister. *(patting sofa)* Bobby? Why don't you come over here and sit with me for a while? *(He does.)* Look there, Bobby. You can see the lights of Gillette. Looks like you could reach right out and touch 'em.

BRENDA. *(Crosses to MICKEY.)* How you doin'?

MICKEY. *(quietly)* The kid is right. Why am I trying to turn this into a home in the suburbs when that's what I've been running away from my whole life? I guess because you start wanting it so early. I was born in this shitty little panhandle town, but there was a time when I thought I was going to find a girl who looked just like Betty on *Father Knows Best*. Incredible, isn't it? I even drove all over town looking for her house, as if there could be such a house in that town. I kept seeing myself going up to the front door, wearing a coat and tie, and there'd be Robert Young. Hello, Mr. Anderson. Hello, Mrs. Anderson. Hello, Bud. I've come to pick up Betty. You know, *belonging*. I kept forgetting I was nothing but a shitkicker through and through.

BRENDA. You know, you sorta remind me of my husband.

MICKEY. You tried it, too?

BRENDA. Sure. Lived in a mobile home in Billings. That's when I was your everyday housewife. Dyed my hair seven different shades of blonde, and he always had a beer in his hand. The neighbors called us Lord Budweiser and Lady Clairol.

MICKEY. What happened?

BRENDA. It got old. But I've got nothing against marriage, in theory.

MICKEY. I've got nothing against it, except it's a life without hope. Once you get married, you got to have coin. Oh, I tried. Got a steady job, managing the Holiday Inn. Shined my shoes, learned to play golf, even joined the First Methodist Church. But I'd lie awake every night thinking: I don't know how much longer I can take this shit. I had only one hope.

BRENDA. What was that?

MICKEY. Publisher's Clearing House. I told my wife: mail every goddamned one of those things in. But I never won, and she left me for a cop.

BRENDA. Got any slow-dancing records?

MICKEY. Floyd Cramer.

BRENDA. That sounds good.

MICKEY. You want to dance?

BRENDA. Sure. *(He puts on Last Date. BRENDA comes into his arms and they circle downstage while BOBBY and CATHY stare up at the starlit sky.)*

CATHY. Just look at those stars.

BOBBY. Like grains of salt on black velvet.

CATHY. They *do* look like salt. You got a real poetic mind, Bobby.

BOBBY. I wish we could go into Gillette. I couldn't wait to get out of there, but now sometimes I look at those lights and feel like there's some kind of party going on, and I should be there. I feel like I'm disappearing out here. I like to have people look at me and wonder who is he? What's he up to? What's he good for? I like making coin, and I like to spend it. I don't think that makes me a fool, do you?

CATHY. No.

BOBBY. I want to be somebody. How are people gonna know who I am, so long as I'm stuck out here?

CATHY. I know just what you mean. When I look up at the stars, I'm always hoping I'll see a UFO. Then somebody could write an article about me for the *National Enquirer.*

BRENDA. *(softly)* How'd you like to go for a walk?

MICKEY. Me?

BRENDA. Who else?

MICKEY. What for?

BRENDA. I want to give you something.

MICKEY. I told you: no money's going to change hands tonight.

BRENDA. This is on the house.

MICKEY. I thought I was striking out with you. Thought I made a fool of myself when I played that record.

BRENDA. You did: that's when I started to like you. Come on. I'm gonna give you something so nice. You're really gonna like it ... *(They stop dancing as song ends.)*

MICKEY. I guess we'll be going for a walk.

BOBBY. *(standing)* All right.

MICKEY. You keep the home fires burning now, you hear?

BOBBY. Sure, hoss. *(MICKEY and BRENDA Exit.)*

CATHY. Boy, she sure changed her tune. But I can see why. You buddy's *beautiful.*

BOBBY. Mickey? But he's got that gray hair and those bags under his eyes. Why, he must be forty years old!

CATHY. Yeah, but for an old dude, he's super cool.

BOBBY. You wouldn't think so if you had to live with him. *(looking in MICKEY'S denim jacket)* If I could only find the keys to the car...

CATHY. Let's just forget about that and enjoy this beautiful night. You guys have got the right idea, living outdoors like this. This is the way people were meant to live.

BOBBY. Yeah. *(sitting again)* Some people think after there's a nuclear war, everybody's gonna be doing it.

CATHY. I know.

BOBBY. You do? *(She nods.)* How?

CATHY. I read all about it in this pamphlet a Jehovah's

Witness gave me. It said nuclear war was the Armageddon predicted in the holy Bible, but it wasn't gonna be so bad. Because after God had cleansed the world of sin with nuclear weapons, everybody was gonna live out in the woods. And it showed these people doing it, and the bears and mountain lions had gotten friendly and were playing with their children just like in *The Wilderness Family*.

BOBBY. What are you, religious or something?

CATHY. I used to be. My family were footwashing pentacostal Baptists. But all the Bible stories gave me impure thoughts. My downfall was a boy named Rodney, who went to our church and looked just like Jesus Christ himself. He had long hair and this sick suffering look. I tried to convert him, and he tried to convert me.

BOBBY. What happened?

CATHY. One night I washed his feet and dried them with my hair, just like the women in the Scriptures. Then he made me holler for the love of the Lord.

BOBBY. *(moving closer)* Cathy ... there's something you could do that would make me so happy. *(Kisses her.)* Is it possible to ... could we...

CATHY. *(forcing him away)* Bobby, let's don't spoil it.

BOBBY. Spoil it?

CATHY. It's been so nice tonight, being treated like a lady. All I've needed for so long was somebody to make me feel like I was worth something. Let's just hold hands.

BOBBY. Unbelievable. *They're* doing it!

CATHY. They're in love, can't you tell?

BOBBY. But you're a hooker! There've been so many!

Would one more make a difference?

CATHY. If that's the way you feel about me, then I'm very disappointed in you, Bobby.

BOBBY. *(groping for billfold)* All right. I'll pay. I've got twenty dollars left—

CATHY. I wouldn't let you do it now for all the money in the world. *(Crosses legs and folds arms defiantly.)* And if you don't behave yourself, I'll yell as loud as I can!

BOBBY. *No!* Don't do that!

CATHY. Are you going to behave yourself?

BOBBY. It's just as well. To tell you the truth. I'm in love with a girl in Gillette — Jody — and I should be true to her. Someday she'll be mine. All I've got to do is get her away from her boyfriend.

CATHY. I hope you do, Bobby.

BOBBY. It's going to be a challenge.

(MICKEY and BRENDA Reenter upstage.)

BOBBY. They're coming! Do me one favor: don't tell Mickey we didn't do it.

CATHY. You're pathetic, aren't you? Just like two little boys showing off for each other.

BOBBY. I'll give you this twenty dollars if you'll keep your mouth shut!

CATHY. All right, it's a deal. *(Takes it.)*

MICKEY. How you doin'?

BOBBY. Fine, fine. I guess *we'll* be going for a walk now.

MICKEY. Yeah, it's real nice over there.

BOBBY. *(pulling CATHY to her feet)* Come on, let's go.

MICKEY. *(whispering to BOBBY as they pass)* You get some?

BOBBY. What do you think?

MICKEY. Where you going now?

BOBBY. To get some more. *(MICKEY socks BOBBY on the arm as he and CATHY Exit. Then he and BRENDA stare silently at each other.)*

BRENDA. That was pretty nice.

MICKEY. Yeah. I can't do it like I could once. But I can do it once like I could pretty often.

BRENDA. I'd say we got off to a good start.

MICKEY. No, this is when it starts. Afterwards.

BRENDA. You're not getting sad, are you?

MICKEY. Why should I? *(picking up bottle)* Know how you feel when you take that first drink after a long time? Like you got a secret or something? A secret you forgot, but it's so good, and you're just about to remember it?

BRENDA. Yeah?

MICKEY. That's how I feel now. *(Puts down bottle.)* But I don't even feel like drinking.

BRENDA. Me either.

(COYOTE howls.)

MICKEY. It's just a coyote. They won't hurt you. *(Sits beside her on sofa, turning on lamp so that they sit in a pool of light, touching her hair.)* You got a secret, Brenda? What's your life about, girl?

BRENDA. I've just got this one problem. I've never found the right man.

MICKEY. You don't need a man. Not a woman like you.

BRENDA. No, but it gets old, going through life alone sometime. *(huddling at the far end of the couch, pulling away from him)* I always know it's gone on too long when I start sleeping in my clothes. Like day or night doesn't matter. Everything goes to shit. I don't ever turn off the light. I just lie down and sleep in my clothes. You've got to watch out for that place.

MICKEY. I hear you.

BRENDA. You've been there, right?

MICKEY. But I'm like you. I keep hoping for the right woman. I keep thinking I'm going to find her.

BRENDA. Where?

MICKEY. *(making light of it)* Under a rock, I don't know. Someplace where I don't expect her, sometime when I'm not looking.

BRENDA. I've given up looking.

MICKEY. No you haven't. Not you.

(COYOTE howls again.)

BRENDA. *(Sits up.)* It's chilly.

MICKEY. Do you mind if I put my arm around you?

BRENDA. No. *(He puts his arm around her and they stare off into the distance.)* The air out here is so clear...

MICKEY. Yeah, you can see a lot from here, and I don't mean just scenery. You look at that town, and you see all the towns that ever were, and every person you've ever been. Long time ago, I decided not to go for the house and kids. I was going for the other dream — freedom and the big score at the end of the road. That's what Gillette was supposed to be for me. Only I forgot what they do to you.

BRENDA. What's that?

MICKEY. *(with growing anger)* They make you work so hard for it you've got nothing left. You change. They get you so you can't think more than one day ahead. Then they throw in all sorts of fun, like dope and girls and video games, that you can't say no to. I've seen Bobby drop fifty dollars a night on those video games, just like he was a child. They *make* you a child. You try to hold on to your coin but spending it's the only thing that makes you feel good anymore.

BRENDA. Like you say, that's every town I've ever been in. Is there someplace better?

MICKEY. Yes there is. Alaska! I'm going to Alaska, where I shoulda gone years ago. I'm gonna score some coin, and this time I'm gonna put a down payment on a fishing boat. I'm gonna see it all before I get too old — bears, icebergs, the Northern Lights, and those big salmon! It's a place so big people got to get bigger to compensate. They get legendary. That's my secret: there's somebody inside me who's bigger and better than I've ever been yet. The Mickey Hollister I was born to be. But when you're in a town, you can't see anymore. And you never recognize the right woman when she comes along, or see your move and know it's time to make it. *(dropping down beside her)* Will you go to Alaska with me?

BRENDA. *(with growing excitement)* Mickey, I've got a cousin in Sitka.

MICKEY. Oh yeah? What does he do?

BRENDA. She. Nothing much, except hunt and fish. She's married to an Aleut. They live on native land. See... I'm an Indian myself. Do you care?

MICKEY. You're an Indian?

BRENDA. A Cree.

MICKEY. Hell, why didn't you say so? I'm one-quarter Oklahoma Cherokee. *(They kiss.)*

BRENDA. How does this sound? We'll go to Anchorage first, and I'll work for you. I can make a lot of money there. Well?

MICKEY. It sounds like a rotten idea.

BRENDA. You think so?

MICKEY. I won't live off a woman. Not when there's the possibility of love here. And it seems to me that there is. You go as my lady or not at all.

BRENDA. *(hugging him)* Oh, I'm so glad you said that. You got me now.

MICKEY. Do I?

BRENDA. You got me now for good and all. *(pulling back)* No, there's one more thing. I got a little girl. She lives with her grandmother in Billings.

MICKEY. She goes too.

BRENDA. If you say so. *(long kiss)* I'm so happy, Mickey.

(Flash of LIGHT.)

BRENDA. What was that?

(Low rumble of THUNDER.)

MICKEY. Holy shit.

BRENDA. It's going to storm.

MICKEY. *(rising)* No it's not. It's not! God won't let me down!

(Rushing sound of FALLING RAIN. BRENDA gives a cry and runs offstage. MICKEY spreads his arms and turns his face to the sky.)

MICKEY. Thank you, God. Thank you for kicking your boy in the ass yet one more time.

SCENE 2

SCENE: The Silver Sollar Lounge, later that night. DOREEN is behind the bar. LEON, a cowboy with a moustache, drinks alone upstage. Downstage, BOOGER and POOT are drinking beer and playing dominos. JODY, who has just taken their order, crosses to the bar.

JODY. Two more Buds.

DOREEN. You got 'em.

JODY. How am I doin'?

DOREEN. Just fine, honey.

(SONNY Enters. Everyone stares at him as he crosses to the bar.)

SONNY. Gimmie a beer.

JODY. I told you not to come here, Sonny.

SONNY. My money's as good as anyone else's, ain't it? *(Throws coins on bar.)* We got to talk.

JODY. If you'll wait a few minutes, maybe I can talk to you.

SONNY. I'm not leaving until you do. *(He drifts over and sits near BOOGER and POOT.)*

JODY. What am I gonna do?

DOREEN. You can take care of yourself, honey. I got lots of confidence in you.

JODY. I hope so. *(She crosses to LEON'S table to take his order.)*

BOOGER. What's the matter, Poot?

POOT. I don't know. I'm sick of drinking here. I'm sick of looking at cowboys. I'm sick of this whole town and everybody in it. I wish I could go back to Texas and lie in the sun.

SONNY. Pardon me, but I couldn't help overhearing your conversation. You're right: these cowboys suck.

POOT. Sure do, buddy.

SONNY. *(moving closer)* Know what just happened to me? I was headed over here on my hog when one of these shitkickers tried to run me off the road. He had a bumper sticker that said *America — Love it or Leave it.* And he was driving a Jap pickup.

POOT. So what?

SONNY. So what? You remember Pearl Harbor, don't you? It was the day the Japs stabbed America in the back. And they're still doing it, every time on of these shitkickers buy a Jap truck. Don't they know American auto workers are going hungry in Detroit?

POOT. I see what he's saying: we should buy American.

SONNY. Only real patriots I ever met were in the joint.

BOOGER. The joint?

SONNY. Yeah, I done a little time. That's where I built my hog — in the prison shop. And it wasn't a Honda, or a Mitsubishi, or a Kawasaki. It was a Harley fucking David-son, the greatest goddamned motorcycle the world has ever known.

BOOGER. I had an old Indian myself once. That were a great scooter.

SONNY. *(encouraged)* You know, I'll bet we've probably got a lot in common. I belonged to this group in prison you guys might be interested in. You ever hear of the Aryan Brotherhood?

BOOGER. Nope, can't say as I have.

SONNY. It's this groups of guys who follow the teaching of Adolph Hitler and the Nazi party. Adolph Hitler's taken a lot of shit from people who don't really know what he stood for, you know?

POOT. He was on the same side as the Japs, wasn't he?

SONNY. Well, yeah, but just because he had to be. I mean, it was him against the whole world.

BOOGER. Well I don't know what else you done while you were in the joint, but you must have spent a lot of time playing with your peter. Because those are the most lunatic ravings I've ever heard.

SONNY. Hey—

BOOGER. Now why don't you just move your ass along and let us drink in peace?

SONNY. All right, all right. *(He crosses away to the bar.)*

BOOGER. Dribbled all his brains right out the end of his peter.

POOT. This town is getting to be full of idiots.

SONNY. *(to JODY: as she returns from LEON'S table)* Jody?

JODY. I'm still busy.

SONNY. I'm in trouble.

JODY. You're always in trouble.

SONNY. Cut me some slack, will you, Jody?

JODY. What is it this time?

SONNY. *(Pulls her to far end of bar, out of hearing of the others.)* The state cops are after me.

JODY. Oh, Sonny...

SONNY. You know that bro I been hanging out with? Big dude they call Dog Breath? Well, last night we got dusted and stuck up a liquor store. We almost got away with it, too. But the dude behind the counter got heavy and chased our asses out of there with a Remington pump.

JODY. You promised me you were going straight.

SONNY. Dog Breath was my sponsor. It's tough being a prospect, Jody. *(proudly)* But now I'm wanted for armed robbery. Now *that's* a really hot beef. I'm going up to Canada, Jody. Tonight. And you're going with me.

JODY. Sonny, I still have a lot of feeling for you. But you have a totally destructive influence on yourself and everyone around you.

SONNY. I know some serious dudes up in Canada,

JODY. they can fix us up with whole new identities. Think of it, Jody. You and me as totally different people.

JODY. I don't want to be somebody else, Sonny. I'm just starting to find out who I am.

SONNY. There you go again! You been giving me this bullshit ever since you run off from me and got this job!

JODY. This job's made a big difference, Sonny. I know I can take care of myself now.

SONNY. But you used to want me to take care of you. *(grabbing her)* I know I promised before, but this tiem I'm gonna change. I love you, baby!

JODY. Get your hands off of me! I'm not taking any more shit, Sonny. Not from you or anybody else!

BOOGER. *(rising)* What's the trouble?

SONNY. No trouble.

BOOGER. *(crossing to them)* Is he bothering you?

SONNY. Why don't you mind your own business, shithead?

JODY. Just make him get out of here and leave me alone!

BOOGER. You heard what the lady said.

SONNY. *Hey! (pulling up jacket to reveal pistol stuck in belt)* I'm packed, motherfucker.

BOOGER. *Besa me Cula.*

SONNY. What's that supposed to mean?

BOOGER. It means kiss my ass in Meskin, and that's exactly what you can do.

SONNY. *(starting to pull gun)* Why you ignorant son-of-a-bitch, I'll blow a hole in you ... *(BOOGER stiff-arms SONNY, knocking him the length of the bar and sending him rolling across the floor. Gun goes flying away. POOT picks it up.)*

BOOGER. I may be an ignorant son-of-a-bitch, but I know one thing: Adolph Hitler was a little turd, and so are you. My daddy fought him, and that's what he told me. And nobody's gonna say my daddy fought on the wrong side — not even some little turd with a gun in his hand. *(advancing on him)* Now get your ass out of my sight before I kick it from here to Odessa.

SONNY. *(picking himself up)* If that's the way you want it, Jody. If that's the way you want it! *(He runs out the door. DOREEN comforts JODY. POOT and LEON crowd around BOOGER, pounding him on the back.)*

POOT. Goddamn, Booger, way to go!

LEON. You done good, big guy. You done real good!

BOOGER. *(glaring at him)* Siddown. *(LEON sits. BOOGER and POOT return to game of dominos.)*

DOREEN. You all right, honey?

JODY. I cared about him. I really did. But I was so afraid I was gonna have to go with him...

DOREEN. Oh, stop it. He was a loser and you know it. Now we're gonna find you a nice young guy with lots of coin.

JODY. I don't know...

DOREEN. Look me in the eye, honey. There's only one question you have to ask yourself: *"Can a Woman Have it All?"* And the answer is *"yes"* — if she lives in Gillette. You are in big demand here, honey. All you've got to do is realize that God has made you a perfect ten, and the rest will take care of itself. Now go fix your face. *(JODY Exits to ladies' room.)*

DOREEN. Booger, let me buy you a beer. In fact, let's everybody have one. *(She crosses to the bar, pours drinks for BOOGER, LEON and POOT.)*

LEON. About time we had some action around here. I was starting to think this place had gone dead.

(Door opens and BOBBY Enters.)

POOT. Well looka here if it ain't Nobis.

BOBBY. Boy, am I glad to see you guys.

POOT. You just missed all the excitement, Nobis. Booger here just showed some asshole it don't pay to mess with oilfield trash.

BOBBY. Look, you guys, I need a favor. Do you think you could loan me some money?

BOOGER. What for?

BOBBY. Mickey smashed up his car. We were having a little party out in the country with these girls when this storm hit and rained us out. So we started back. Mickey was driving too fast, and he hit a rock and broke the axle.

POOT. Anybody hurt?

BOBBY. Mickey got a bump on the head. The girls are taking care of him. I hitchhiked back here to get a tow truck. I've been to every filling station in town and they all want a deposit.

BOOGER. So Hollister's in trouble, huh? Well, I tried to help him out once and he wouldn't go for it.

BOBBY. But Booger, they're waiting for me. All I need is twenty dollars.

BOOGER. Hollister's smart as a tack. He can bullshit his

way out of anything. Let him bullshit his way out of this.

BOBBY. You mean I've got to hitchhike back out there in the rain and tell them you wouldn't help?

BOOGER. I guess you do.

BOBBY. It's forty miles back out there!

BOOGER. Tough titty, Nobis. *(They laugh.)*

BOBBY. Well, thanks for nothing.

(He starts to go. Then crosses to one of the computer games, drops in a coin, starts playing. JODY Reenters.)

JODY. Bobby?

BOBBY. Jody...

JODY. I had a feeling I might be seeing you again. I got something here that belongs to you. *(She takes guitar out from behind bar and crosses to him.)* I wouldn't let Sonny sell it.

BOBBY. I appreciate it, Jody.

JODY. You gonna be here for a minute? I'd like to talk to you.

BOBBY. Let's talk. *(They sit at table downstage.)* How long you been workin' here?

JODY. Ever since I left Sonny. I'm living with Doreen now — she got me this job — he's on his way to Canada.

BOBBY. Ain't you worried? Who's gonna protect you if there's a nuclear war while he's gone?

JODY. Don't make fun of me, Bobby. Sometimes I can't sleep for thinking about it. But it got so I was more afraid of Sonny than I was of it, so I left him. And it's been better since I got this job. I mean, these people like me. You can't believe how much money I'm making, and I don't even have to do anything except smile a lot. It's totally incredible to me, because this is the first job I've ever had. If I'd known it was this easy, I'd of gone to work a long time ago.

BOBBY. Everybody's got to get out on their own sometime, Jody.

JODY. I found out there's all sorts of things I can do. I can cut people's hair. *(touching his hair)* Yours is getting pretty long. Come see me sometime, and maybe I'll give you a trim.

BOBBY. Maybe I will.

JODY. So what have you been doing with yourself, Bobby?

BOBBY. Living way out in the sticks with my buddy, Mickey. I was so lonesome out there I almost died. I really looked up to Mickey, but now I just feel sorry for him. He's got nothing and he's going nowhere. But I'm coming back to this town and I'm gonna do what I said: make some big coin and write my songs.

JODY. I'm glad Bobby. But hey — I feel like shit I let Sonny nail you to that floor.

BOBBY. Something I got to know, Jody.

JODY. What's that?

BOBBY. Why'd you stay with him so long? Did you really love him that much? *(She avoids his eye.)* No bullshit, now Jody?

JODY. It was stay with him or get the shit beaten out of me. You ever get the shit beaten out of you, Bobby? You know what that's like? First time it happened, Sonny cried like a baby, and promised he'd never do it again. And he was so nice to me afterward, nicer than he's ever been.

BOBBY. You sound like you enjoyed it.

JODY. I didn't enjoy getting *hit,* stupid! *(pause)* I guess I did enjoy forgiving him. You think, I'm not like one of those stupid women on the Phil Donahue show. I mean, they've got a problem, they're really sick. But before you know it, you're caught in the same trap. None of us are as smart as we think we are, Bobby, that's what I'm saying. *(She starts away.)*

BOBBY. *(stopping her)* Jody! *(She lets him hold her.)* I've been waiting a long time for that.

DOREEN. Honey, it's getting late. Why don't you go on home?

JODY. Don't you want me to help you close out?

DOREEN. I can take care of it.

BOBBY. It was good talking to you, Jody.

JODY. Bobby, were you going someplace? Because I'm thinking I might have trouble sleeping tonight.

BOBBY. No ... I wasn't going anyplace.

JODY. You could come back to my place ... and maybe I could give you that haircut.

BOBBY. I'd like that Jody.

JODY. So would I.

SCENE 3

*SCENE: A laundromat, on the following night. Harsh fluorescent
LIGHT. MICKEY slumped on a row of green plastic chairs,
his belongings in a shopping bag. BRENDA Enters, carry-
ing another shopping bag full of bottles.*

BRENDA. Our troubles are over. Look what I found.

MICKEY. What?

BRENDA. Bottles. I was out collecting 'em along the
side of the road. There's a nickel deposit on each one. It's
not a fortune, but maybe it'll buy us a cup of coffee. *(when
he shoves the bag away)* Come on, Mickey. Don't be this
way. We've still got each other.

MICKEY. Yeah. And we got a nice warm laundromat to
spend the night in. If the cops don't kick up us out.

BRENDA. *(taking bottle out of bag)* I used to do this when I
was a little girl. Collected bottles. Except they were different bottles then. Royal Crown Cola. Bubble Up.
Delaware Punch. *(Looks at him.)* Did you find Bobby?

MICKEY. No. *(taking bottle of Wild Turkey from bag, drinking)* I can't believe that son-of-a-bitch would run off with
the last of our coin.

BRENDA. How do you think I feel about Cathy catching
that bus to Laramie? We were supposed to be
partners too.

MICKEY. You can't trust nobody.

BRENDA. I wonder where she got that twenty dollars?

74

MICKEY. Someday I'm gonna see him again. And when I do, I'm gonna teach him a lesson he'll never forget.

BRENDA. *(Pauses, then.)* Mickey, there's a way out of this.

MICKEY. What.

BRENDA. I could find a customer.

MICKEY. Don't say it! Don't even think it! You do that, girl, and you lost me. Forever!

BRENDA. Well, we've got to do something. We've been here all day now. I can't take this any longer.

MICKEY. You can if I say so.

BRENDA. You're starting to sound like my husband.

MICKEY. You're starting to look like my wife. *(crossing to change machine)* Maybe this thing's got some coin in it. *(trying to pry it open with pocketknife)* Everything was going just fine until that storm hit...

BRENDA. Well, you should of known you couldn't just live out there like that forever. Sooner or later the weather was gonna change.

MICKEY. Pretty goddamned funny, wasn't it? All my belongings, my clothes, my records, blown to hell and gone. *(Takes record out of jacket.)* One record — that's all I've got left!

BRENDA. Who cares about your records? If only you hadn't totalled your car.

MICKEY. Yeah, well I don't feel so hot about that either.

BRENDA. I told you you were driving too fast.

MICKEY. *(banging on change machine)* Lay off of me, will you? Just lay off!

BRENDA. But that was the car we were supposed to go

to Alaska in! And now we're stuck in a laundromat, and you don't have a job, and I'm out collecting pop bottles!

MICKEY. Maybe I like it here! Maybe I'm getting used to it!

BRENDA. Oh, Mickey, Alaska was just a lot of talk, wasn't it? A lot of hot air is all it was. But I wanted to believe it.

MICKEY. *(softly)* So did I. I don't know, girl. I thought you were my ghost shirt or something. Ain't that what they called 'em? Those shirts the Indians wore that were supposed to be bulletproof?

BRENDA. Yeah.

MICKEY. So the braves put them on and rode out to meet the cavalry, shouting their defiance. A wonderful thing. An Indian thing. *(bitterly, turning away)* 'Course it was all just a lot of stone age bullshit. Big medicine. Nine times out of ten, a brave would go there in his ghost shirt and get greased. The Indians had a lot of spirit. But they always lost. *(Slumps in chair, drinks.)*

BRENDA. *(watching him)* Yeah. Indians are losers. Mickey?

MICKEY. Yeah?

BRENDA. Are you gonna marry me?

MICKEY. *(startled)* Right now?

BRENDA. Why not?

MICKEY. We ain't got a nickel.

BRENDA. I know.

MICKEY. These things need planning ... and a lot of thought. What sort of honeymoon could we have?

BRENDA. But you said we had love here.

MICKEY. I said the *possibility* of love...

BRENDA. *(turning away)* then I'm gonna find a customer.

MICKEY. I've got my *pride*...

BRENDA. I don't.

MICKEY. Go on then! Peddle your ass in every boom town in Wyoming! See if I care! *(kicking bag)* And take your goddamned bottles with you!

BRENDA. You're disappearing on me, Mickey.

MICKEY. I ain't disappearing, girl! You are!

BRENDA. You're right. *(Takes bottle from him, drinks.)* Soon as I turn this trick, I'm catching the next bus out of here. I'm going to Billings, to get my little girl. Then I'm gonna take her to the Res to meet her grandfather. We'll go to that little shack with the turtle shell nailed over the door. I'll bring him a bottle of peach brandy and some peanut butter cups. We'll sit and watch the moon rise. And he'll teach her to want ... nothing. *(when he doesn't respond)* Goodbye, Mickey.

MICKEY. Brenda ... *(but she has already gone)*

SCENE 4

SCENE: *The Silver Dollar Lounge, later that night. DOREEN behind the bar, LEON and two other customers drinking. BRENDA is sitting at a table downstage when lights come up JODY is standing beside it, waiting to take her order.*

BRENDA. You know how to make a Rusty Nail?

JODY. That's Scotch and Drambuie, right?

BRENDA. Right. *(JODY crosses to bar.)*

DOREEN. Jody, you and I have got to have a talk.

JODY. Just let me serve this drink and I'll be right with you. *(crossing back to BRENDA with drink)* I haven't seen you in here before.

BRENDA. It's my first time. Mind if I ask you something?

JODY. No.

BRENDA. How much do you make here?

JODY. The pay's not so great, but I make about a hundred dollars a night in tips. Anything else you need to know?

BRENDA. How old are you?

JODY. Nineteen.

BRENDA. Nineteen. Jesus.

JODY. Could I ask you something?

BRENDA. Sure.

JODY. What do you do?

BRENDA. What do you think I do?

JODY. I think you're a hooker.

BRENDA. Yeah. It's no big secret. That's what I do.

JODY. I'm not supposed to let you stay here. It's bad for the atmosphere.

BRENDA. You gonna throw me out?

LEON. *(who has crossed to them)* You want to dance?

BRENDA. No thanks.

LEON. I'll buy you a drink.

BRENDA. I've already got a drink.

LEON. Goodlooking woman like you shouldn't be

alone on a Saturday night.

JODY. Leave her alone, Leon. Can't you see she doesn't want to be bothered?

LEON. Who says I'm bothering her?

JODY. Leave her alone or I'll have to ask you to go.

BRENDA. Maybe later, honey.

LEON. Shitfire ... *(He drifts back to the bar.)*

JODY. What was wrong with him?

BRENDA. I'm not drunk enough yet.

JODY. Look, you can stay for a while.

BRENDA. Thanks.

JODY. *(Crosses back to bar. To DOREEN:)* What is it?

DOREEN. That boy you brought home last night? When I went back just now, he was still there. He was standing there in the middle of the kitchen floor, wearing my bathrobe and eating our meatloaf.

JODY. I'm sorry, Doreen.

DOREEN. I don't want to be shitty about this, but a woman's got to have her space. He moves in, there goes my space. Next thing you know, we've got trouble with the landlord.

JODY. I'll tell him he's got to go.

DOREEN. I don't suppose he's got a job?

JODY. He's looking for work.

DOREEN. Jody, how many times do I have to tell you? You got to find yourself a high roller.

JODY. It's just not very romantic.

DOREEN. Honey, if I want romance, I'll read *Sweet Savage Love* or watch the soaps. That's what they're for.

(BOBBY Enters.)

DOREEN. Here he is now. Do your thing, honey. *(Moves away as BOBBY approaches.)*

BOBBY. Jody, what's the deal? Your roommate threw me out.

JODY. Bobby, I told you you couldn't stay.

BOBBY. That was *before* we spent the night together.

JODY. Bobby? Are you sure you didn't come home with me because you needed a place to stay?

BOBBY. How can you think that?

JODY. Suppose I did let you stay. You haven't got a job.

BOBBY. You didn't care if I had a job last night.

JODY. But Bobby, you might become dependent on me. First thing I know, you'd be hanging around all day instead of going out and looking for one. Which is to say I found you really hot last night. But if you expect me to cook and clean and wash your dirty Jockey shorts for you, I just might not find you totally sexy forever!

BOBBY. Jody, I think I love you.

JODY. Oh no, none of that! I've been in love half my young life. I don't need any more love right now, thank you!

BOBBY. All right, Jody. I'll go out first thing in the morning and I'll find a job, I promise. Even if it's washing dishes.

JODY. That's good, Bobby. Because every time some guy tells me he loves me, I always end up taking care of him. I don't know why, but I'm not gonna let it happen again. *(She turns away. BOBBY watches LEON cross to*

BRENDA'S table, sees her for the first time.)

LEON. Waiting for somebody else? Maybe they ain't coming.

BRENDA. Maybe not.

LEON. *(sitting)* You know, I used to like *Dallas*. But I just can't watch that show since Jock Ewing died.

BRENDA. Look, you don't have to talk to me. Just buy me a drink. *(LEON crosses to bar, BOBBY crosses to BREN-DA'S table.)*

BOBBY. Brenda?

BRENDA. *(doesn't recognize him, then)* Oh yeah. How you doin', kid?

BOBBY. Where's Mickey?

BRENDA. I don't know. I left him in a laundromat, feeling sorry for himself. *(Drinks.)* He's been looking for you.

BOBBY. Has he?

BRENDA. He said when he found you, he was going to teach you a lesson you'd never forget.

(MICKEY Enters, sees them.)

BOBBY. I'd better go find him. I've got a lot of explaining to do. *(Turns, finds himself face to face with MICKEY.)*

MICKEY. You...

BOBBY. Mickey...

MICKEY. Where in the hell have you been?

BOBBY. I got something to tell you, Mickey.

MICKEY. Where's our money?

BOBBY. I lost our money, Mickey. But I found Jody.

MICKEY. Jody?

BOBBY. *(indicating JODY)* She works here.

MICKEY. Oh, that's great. You were shacked up with a hot young thing, and my lady and I were spending the night n a laundromat.

BOBBY. She's more than that, Mickey. She's a lot more.

MICKEY. You run out on me, son. I never would have run out on you. You shoulda been a better friend to me.

BOBBY. I can't live like you any more, Mickey! I want four walls and I want that girl, and I'm gonna get her.

MICKEY. You're an ignorant little shithead, and I wish to God I'd never laid eyes on you! Now get out of my sight before I beat the living shit out of you. *(BOBBY crosses back to bar. MICKEY sits at BRENDA'S table.)* There's some things that shouldn't be sold. Some things that are worth more than coin. You do this and you're selling our love. And it's precious, girl. Once it's gone, you can't ever buy it back.

BRENDA. I need the *money*.

MICKEY. I'll get us some money, somehow. I will. You've got to give me more time!

LEON. *(crossing back to table with drinks)* What's going on, honey? I thought you liked me?

MICKEY. *(rising)* She changed her mind.

BRENDA. Clear out of here, Mickey. The man's buying me a drink...

MICKEY. *(to LEON: taking record out of jacket)* How'd you like to buy a record?

LEON. What?

MICKEY. I got a record here. Not just any record, but a

priceless original recording of Roy Orbison singing *It's Over* — signed by the great Roy Orbison himself.

LEON. No shit?

MICKEY. *(dragging him toward bar)* Why don't you just come on over here, where you can get a better look at it. See? Right there on the label. His signature. This record can't be bought in any store, but I'm forced to sell it right here and now, tonight, for the ridiculously low price of only two hundred dollars.

LEON. Two hundred dollars? What the hell you trying to pull?

MICKEY. *(to the room:)* Why this record is worth two or three hundred times that. See for yourself. He signed it one night in Lubbock, in the year 1962. Remember those days? Your first girl? She was so innocent — and so were you. You didn't know how much she meant to you, until one day, in a careless moment, you treated her badly. And she turned her back on you. Left you for the captain of the football team. *(looking at BRENDA)* And when she did, you realized that her love meant more to you than anything in the world. That if she loved you, there was nothing you couldn't do. You begged her to come back — but it was too late. You were all alone. And you played this record. That's what I told Roy, and that's when he signed it "with deepest regrets, Roy Orbison."

CUSTOMER. Shit, I'll give you five bucks for it.

LEON. I'll give you twenty.

MICKEY. I'll let it go for fifty. But it's a sacrifice.

DOREEN. Leon, you pay fifty dollars for that record, and you're even dumber than I thought. *(Everyone laughs.)*

LEON. Sorry, buddy. forget it. *(Goes back to BRENDA's table. Customers turn their backs on MICKEY.)*

MICKEY. But it's all here on this record. Precious memories of a time when we loved. A time before we lost it. *It's Over! (when no one responds)* I guess it is. Nobody wants to buy this precious record? Fine. Go fuck yourselves.

(BOOGER and JEETER Enter.)

BOOGER. What do you say, Hollister? *(to DOREEN:)* Give me a shot of Jim Beam. In fact, give everybody a shot. Drinks are on me. *(Everybody crowds around bar.)*

JODY. What's the occasion?

BOOGER. We're drinking to Poot McCullough. He was throwing the chain and got pulled into the cathead. Tore him up something awful. We met Jeeter here when we were bringing him back to town.

JEETER. I turned on my siren and we done ninety all the way to the hospital.

BOOGER. Poot McCullough was the best worker I ever knowed. I wish I played ball with him. It would have been a privilege. *(Raises glass.)* To Poot.

ALL. To Poot. *(They drink.)*

BOOGER. Son-of-a-bitch left me in a hell of a spot, though, I need four hands on the floor for the eight o'clock shift, and now I'm one man short.

MICKEY. I want that job!

BOBBY. I want that job!

BOOGER. I thought you didn't care to work for me, Hollister.

MICKEY. Things are different now. *(pointing to BRENDA)* I got a woman with a kid to support. You know I've got the experience.

BOBBY. Give a young guy a chance, Booger.

BOOGER. As I recollect, you didn't care to work for me either, Nobis.

BOBBY. I've changed, Booger. I've seen the light.

MICKEY. Don't listen to this kid!

BOBBY. Maybe I'm just a kid, but I can do ten times the work you can.

MICKEY. I ain't so old I can't whip your young ass.

BOOGER. *(grinning)* If you boys want the job so bad, I guess you'll have to fight for it.

MICKEY. Suits me.

BOBBY. Go for it.

BOOGER. *(shouting)* All right, who wants to see two men fight for a job? They'll pound the shit out of each other before your very eyes, and whoever's still standing when it's over goes to work for me! *(CUSTOMER'S roar approval.)*

DOREEN. No, Booger, they'll bust the place up!

JEETER. There ain't gonna be any fighting here tonight, Booger.

BOOGER. Why not?

JEETER. I'm a deputy sheriff of Campbell County, that's why. If there's a fight, I got to arrest these boys for disturbing the peace.

BOOGER. It'd give me a lot of personal satisfaction to see these boys fight. *(taking out billfold)* I'll pay for the damages.

JEETER. That's not the point. It ain't legal. If these boys

fight, they're going to jail.

BOOGER. But I need one of 'em to work for me.

JEETER. I got to enforce the law.

BOOGER. *(Takes him aside.)* They don't both got to go to jail, do they? Why not just take the loser? *(Gives him money.)*

JEETER. Fighting for a job, huh? I'd like to see that myself. *(to the room:)* All right, what the hell: they fight, and the loser goes to jail! *(CROWD responds, begins to move tables back to make room for fight.)*

BRENDA. For Christ's sake, Mickey, be careful. *(Everyone gathers around the dance floor, where BOBBY, who has taken off his shirt, and MICKEY, who has rolled up his sleeves, face each other in a pool of light from the overhead lamp. BOOGER steps between them.)*

BOOGER. All right, gentlemen, what's it gonna be tonight? Oil patch rules?

BOBBY. What's oil patch rules?

MICKEY. Anything goes.

BOOGER. That's how it's done. This ain't no golden gloves, you know.

BOBBY. All right. Anything goes.

JODY. Put him away, Bobby. You can do it!

BOOGER. *(announcer's voice)* In this corner, the fighting dog of the oil patch, never yet lost a battle. A fighting machine who knows every dirty hold. And in this corner, the young comer, the golden boy. Watch him carefully folks, he's liable to surprise you tonight. Here's the bell for round one!

(DOREEN bangs a tray. CUSTOMERS form a circle around

BOBBY and MICKEY who circle cautiously, throwing punches that don't connect.)

BOOGER. They're at the center of the ring, they're feeling each other out. A lot rests on this match. Hollister's got his guard up, he feints, the kid's too fast for him. Now the kid feints. The crowd is disappointed. These boys seem to think this is a dancing school or something. What the hell, you gonna fight, or hug and kiss? This ain't Arthur Murray, you're supposed to giving us some thrills tonight!

(CUSTOMERS grows impatient. LEON shoves BOBBY into MICKEY. They grapple. CUSTOMERS close in, and for a moment nothing can be seen. Then they part and MICKEY and BOBBY, still struggling sink to the floor, exhausted. CROWD NOISE dies and they face each other in the pool of light.)

MICKEY. You sure you want it, son? It ain't no life.
BOBBY. No, but I got to have it.
MICKEY. Then this is your last lesson.
BOBBY. You been a good teacher, Mickey.
MICKEY. I ain't gonna go easy on you.
BOBBY. I wouldn't want you to. Finally they get you in a corner where it's friendship or coin, don't they? Then you got to take the coin and fuck your friends.
MICKEY. Son, you have just become a working man.
BOBBY. Have I?
MICKEY. You have graduated with flying colors.
BOBBY. *(helping him to his feet)* No hard feelings?
MICKEY. No hard feelings. *(MICKEY hits BOBBY with a*

*left hook that drops him unconscious to the floor. MICKEY opens
his fist. Coins from the broken roll of nickels concealed in his fist
drop to the floor. MICKEY turns to BRENDA, who gives him his
hard hat, then to BOOGER.)* Let's go to work.

(They move toward the door as the stage DARKENS.)

AUTHOR'S NOTE

Plays take a long time to write, and for some reason this one always had to do with travelling. I first saw the town of Gillette at the age of five, when my father, a geologist, was mapping the Thunder Basin. We drove through one afternoon on our way to somewhere else. In 1981, while driving across the country, I passed through a Utah boom town, and later wrote one of the scenes as a short story. I began it as a play in 1984, at a time when I was often going back to Texas. Large portions of the first draft were written in a departure lounge at DFW.

This play is not about the "myth of the West," but about real people and real conditions that existed in Gillette at the time of the boom. If there are myths here, they are the myths of the big score and the good ole' boy. To be a good ole' boy is to be forever young and irresponsible—a role that directly denies the realities of working class life. Still, that's about all the working man's got. Mickey, for instance, is a gifted guy, but his only outlet is to be the world's greatest good ole' boy. What does that get you when you're forty? Not much. When I was once asked to describe this play, I called it "a comedy of disillusionment." My intent was to write about serious concerns with humor, like the best country music does.

A strange thing happened during the evolution of this play. When I wrote the first draft, the Roy Orbison revival hadn't even begun. While it was being produced, he was famous again. A few days after I turned in the script to Samuel French, he died. This play is dedicated to him, to a lot of good ole' boys I grew up with in Wichita Falls, Texas — itself a boom town — and to every member of every cast of *Gillette,* without whose contributions I could not have completed it.

COSTUME PLOT

MICKEY HOLLISTER:
ACT I, 1
> Faded straight leg jeans
> Printed, faded dress-style shirt
> Jean jacket, classic Levi style
> T-shirt
> Black, dusty cowboy boots
> Tooled leather belt with vanity buckle

ACT I, 3
> Work boots
> Faded, oily straight leg jeans
> Green Haynes T-shirt
> Faded blue work shirt
> Red "trucker's" cap with logo

ACT I, 5/6
> Red Haynes T-shirt
> Tan stained coveralls open to waist and sleeves rolled
> Red hard hat
> Brown stained work boots

ACT II, 1
> Black cowboy boots (as in I/1)
> Jeans, straight leg (as in I/1)

Black denim pearl snap western style shirt
Blue sharkskin one-button tuxedo dinner jacket

ACT II, 3/4

Same as above without tux jacket
Add jean jacket seen in I/1

BOBBY NOBIS:

ACT I, 1

Flare leg (boot-style) jeans
"Aerosmith" T-shirt
Plaid flannel shirt, worn out, unbuttoned, sleeves
rolled up
Tooled leather belt
Brown, dusty cowboy boots
Straw cowboy hat

ACT I, 3

New black flare Levis with price tags (rigged for
nails)
New two-tone high-heeled cowboy boots
New white high-crown Stetson cowboy hat
New black tooled leather western belt with large
buckle
Black and turquoise western shirt with snap but
tons
Pale used western shirt (rigged for nails)

ACT I, 5/6

Faded, oil-stained jeans
"Alabama" T-shirt

        Oil-stained flannel shirt, sleeves cut off
        Red "trucker's" cap
        Brown, stained work shoes

ACT II, 1
        Two-tone cowboy boots as in I,3
        Faded straight leg Levis
        Black and turquoise western shirt as in I, 3
        Black western belt as in I, 3

ACT II, 2
        Same as above, with brown leather zipper jacket

ACT II, 4
        Same as above, no jacket

DOREEN:
ACT I, 1
        Pink plastic rollers covered with aqua chiffon
           scarf
        White plastic earrings
        Tight-fitting knit shell, push-up bra
        Chamois-colored tight jeans
        Pink and wood high-heeled "candies"

ACT II, 2
        Tight-fitting turquoise angora sweater
        Tight jeans
        Knee-high cowgirl boots with high heels
        Large pink earrings

ACT II, 4

>White jeans with rhinestone and black stitching
>   on pockets
>Matching white jacket with black fringe and
>   front zipper
>Black high-heeled cowgirl boots
>Earrings

BRENDA:
ACT I, 2

>Hot pink polyester halter minidress
>Chubby waist-length rabbit jacket
>Indian necklace
>Black oversized shoulder bag
>Black high-heeled knee-high side-zippered boots

ACT I, 4

>Tangerine cotton hospital style "scrub suit,"
>   stencilled front, back and trouser leg with
>   "Campbell County"
>Rubber shower thongs

ACT II, 1

>Red polyester dress, similar to Act I, 2
>Same boots as in I, 2
>Same jacket as in I, 2
>Same bag as in I, 2
>Jewelry as in I, 2

ACT II, 3/4

>Same as II, 1, but distressed

CATHY:

ACT I, 2

    Bluejean miniskirt
    White western belt
    Peach tube top
    Pink studded jean vest
    White and pink high-heeled cowgirl boots
    Feather earrings
    Metallic shoulder bag

ACT I, 4

    Tangerine cotton hospital-style "scrub suit." stencilled front, back, and trouser leg with "Campbell County."
    Rubber shower thongs

ACT II, 1

    Skirt as in I, 2
    Vest as in I, 2
    Boots as in I, 2
    Bag as in I, 2
    Shocking pink lycra leotard

JEETER:

ACT I, 2

    Beige polyester-cotton western style shirt
    Brown and white print polyester shirt open at neck
    Pukka beads
    Brown western belt with large shiny buckle
    Brown high-heeled cowboy boots
    Beige cowboy hat, high-crowned

ACT II, 4

> Tan flared trousers, same belt as in I, 2
> Navy blue and orange polyester shirt, open at neck
> Brown leather "flight-style" jacket with front zipper
> Tan Stetson cowboy hat

JODY:

ACT I, 3

> Suede fringed skimpy halter top
> Very cut-off jean shorts
> Black short leather jacket
> Blue suede very high spike-heeled boots
> Fringe earrings

ACT II, 2

> Rayon print blouse
> Designer style "baggie" jeans
> Cowgirl boots
> Earrings
> Neck chain with heart

ACT II, 4

> Pink shiny leotard top with long sleeves
> Choker necklace
> Same jeans as II, 2
> Same boots as II, 2
> Earrings

SONNY:
ACT I, 2
>   Black sleeveless Harley Davidson T-shirt
>   Black leather snap front vest with emblems
>   Dirty jeans with soiled knees and seat
>   Black leather engineer boots
>   Black leather wallet attached to pants with chain
>   Black leather belt, Harley buckle
>   Tattoos

ACT II, 2
>   Same as above, with addition of black leather
>   motorcycle jacket

BOOGER McCOY:
ACT I, 1
>   Oil-atained tan coveralls with sleeves cut off,
>   worn over:
>   Dirty blue short-sleeved T-shirt
>   Scuffed hard hat
>   Oily work boots
>   Oily, dirty work gloves

ACT I, 5
>   Faded plaid flannel shirt with sleeves rolled up
>   Quilted work vest
>   Tan work pants
>   Brown work boots
>   White hard hat

ACT II, 2
>Polyester "flare leg" dress pants
>Polyester landscape-printed shirt
>Worn-out trousers
>Dark brown leather jacket
>Black side-buckle leather shoes

ACT II, 4
>Same as I, 1, with Sears bluejean work jacket with corduroy collar

POOT:
ACT I, 1
>Blue-gray coveralls, stained and oily, open to waist
>Stained and oily work boots
>Scuffed hard hat

ACT I, 5
>Same stained coveralls as in 1
>Black T-shirt
>Black "trucker's" cap
>Brown work shoes

ACT II, 2
>"Designer" dress jeans with fancy stitching on back pockets
>Black "Southern Pride" T-shirt
>Imitation tan leather sport jacket
>Black "trucker's" cap

CHIGGER:
ACT I, 5
     Plaid flannel shirt with sleeves cut off
     Tan oil-stained coveralls with sleeves cut off
     Stained brown work boots
     Yellow hard hat
     Dark-tinted safety glasses

LEON:
ACT II, 2/4
     Plaid western shirt
     Brown suede western-style vest
     Jeans
     Cowboy hat
     Cowboy boots
     Belt with large buckle

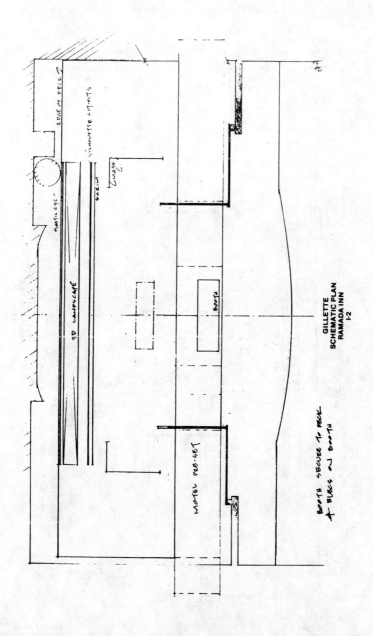

GILLETTE
SCHEMATIC PLAN
RAMADA INN
I-2

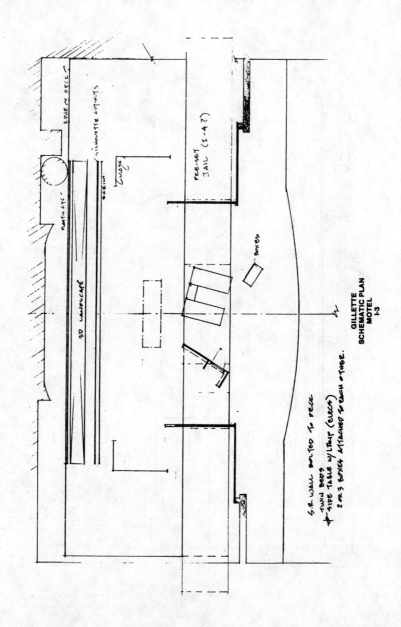

GILLETTE
SCHEMATIC PLAN
MOTEL
I-3

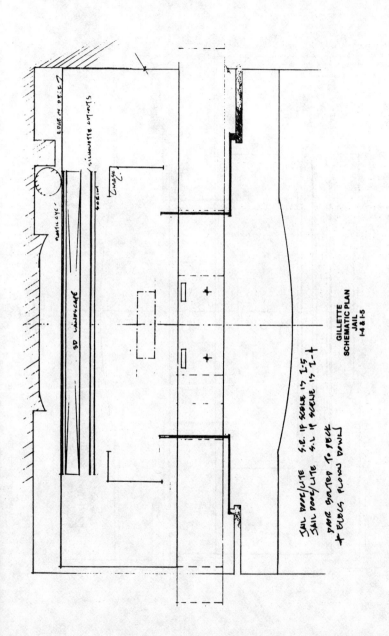

GILLETTE
SCHEMATIC PLAN
JAIL
I-4 & I-5

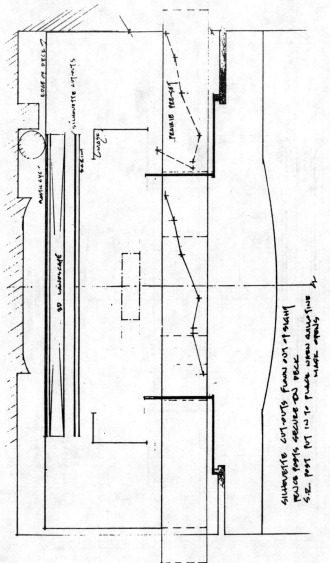

GILLETTE
SCHEMATIC PLAN
PRAIRIE FENCE
1-8

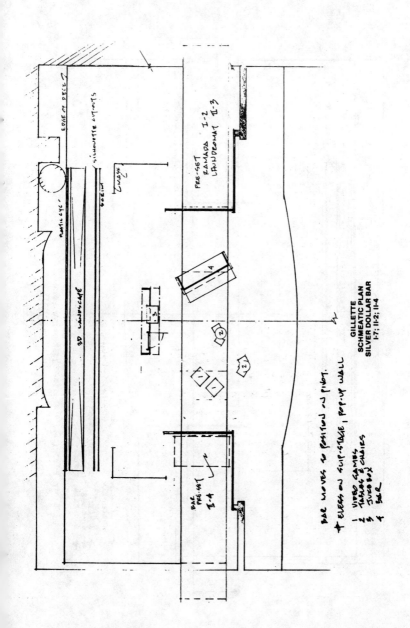

GILLETTE
SCHMEATIC PLAN
SILVER DOLLAR BAR
I-7; II-2; II-4

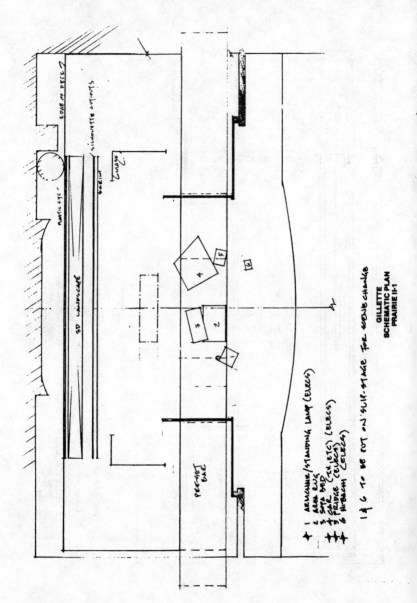

GILLETTE
SCHEMATIC PLAN
PRAIRIE II-1

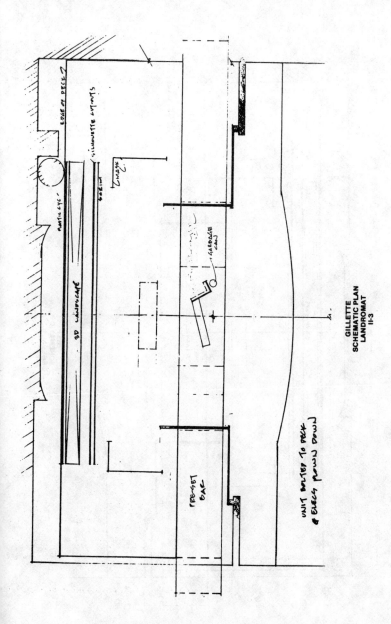

GILLETTE
SCHEMATIC PLAN
LANDROMAT
II-3

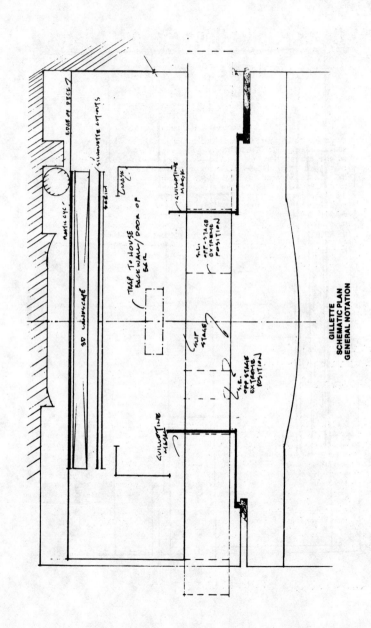

GILLETTE
SCHEMATIC PLAN
GENERAL NOTATION

Other Publications for Your Interest

AGNES OF GOD
(LITTLE THEATRE—DRAMA)

By JOHN PIELMEIER

3 women—1 set (bare stage)

Doctor Martha Livingstone, a court-appointed psychiatrist, is asked to determine the sanity of a young nun accused of murdering her own baby. Mother Miriam Ruth, the nun's superior, seems bent on protecting Sister Agnes from the doctor, and Livingstone's suspicions are immediately aroused. In searching for solutions to various mysteries (who killed the baby? Who fathered the child?) Livingstone forces all three women, herself included, to face some harsh realities in their own lives, and to re-examine the meaning of faith and the commitment of love. "Riveting, powerful, electrifying new drama . . . three of the most magnificent performances you will see this year on any stage anywhere . . . the dialogue crackles."—Rex Reed, N.Y. Daily News. ". . . outstanding play . . . deals intelligently with questions of religion and psychology."—Mel Gussow, N.Y. Times. ". . . unquestionably blindingly theatrical . . . cleverly executed blood and guts evening in the theatre . . . three sensationally powered performances calculated to wring your withers."—Clive Barnes, N.Y. Post.   (#236)

COME BACK TO THE 5 & DIME, JIMMY DEAN, JIMMY DEAN
(ADVANCED GROUPS—DRAMA)

By ED GRACZYK

1 man, 8 women—Interior

In a small-town dime store in West Texas, the Disciples of James Dean gather for their twentieth reunion. Now a gaggle of middle-aged women, the Disciples were teenagers when Dean filmed "Giant" two decades ago in nearby Marfa. One of them, an extra in the film, has a child whom she says was conceived by Dean on the "Giant" set; the child is the Jimmy Dean of the title. The ladies' reminiscences mingle with flash-backs to their youth; then the arrival of a stunning and momentarily unrecognized woman sets off a series of confrontations that upset their self-deceptions and expose their well-hidden disappointments. "Full of homespun humor . . . surefire comic gems."—N.Y. Post. "Captures convincingly the atmosphere of the 1950s."—Women's Wear Daily.   (#5147)

Other Publications for Your Interest

A WEEKEND NEAR MADISON
(LITTLE THEATRE—COMIC DRAMA)
By KATHLEEN TOLAN

2 men, 3 women—Interior

This recent hit from the famed Actors Theatre of Louisville, a terrific ensemble play about male-female relationships in the 80's, was praised by *Newsweek* as "warm, vital, glowing . . . full of wise ironies and unsentimental hopes". The story concerns a weekend reunion of old college friends now in their early thirties. The occasion is the visit of Vanessa, the queen bee of the group, who is now the leader of a lesbian/feminist rock band. Vanessa arrives at the home of an old friend who is now a psychiatrist hand in hand with her naif-like lover, who also plays in the band. Also on hand are the psychiatrist's wife, a novelist suffering from writer's block; and his brother, who was once Vanessa's lover and who still loves her. In the course of the weekend, Vanessa reveals that she and her lover desperately want to have a child—and she tries to persuade her former male lover to father it, not understanding that he might have some feelings about the whole thing. *Time Magazine* heard "the unmistakable cry of an infant hit . . . Playwright Tolan's work radiates promise and achievement." (#25051)

PASTORALE
(LITTLE THEATRE—COMEDY)
By DEBORAH EISENBERG

3 men, 4 women—Interior
(plus 1 or 2 bit parts and 3 optional extras)

"Deborah Eisenberg is one of the freshest and funniest voices in some seasons."—Newsweek. Somewhere out in the country Melanie has rented a house and in the living room she, her friend Rachel who came for a weekend but forgets to leave, and their school friend Steve (all in their mid-20s) spend nearly a year meandering through a mental landscape including such concerns as phobias, friendship, work, sex, slovenliness and epistemology. Other people happen by: Steve's young girlfriend Celia, the virtuous and annoying Edie, a man who Melanie has picked up in a bar, and a couple who appear during an intense conversation and observe the sofa is on fire. The lives of the three friends inevitably proceed and eventually draw them, the better prepared perhaps by their months on the sofa, in separate directions. "The most original, funniest new comic voice to be heard in New York theater since Beth Henley's 'Crimes of the Heart.'"—N.Y. Times. "A very funny, stylish comedy."—The New Yorker. "Wacky charm and wayward wit."—New York Magazine. "Delightful."—N.Y. Post. "Uproarious . . . the play is a world unto itself, and it spins."—N.Y. Sunday Times. (#18016)

Other Publications for Your Interest

HUSBANDRY
(LITTLE THEATRE—DRAMA)
By PATRICK TOVATT

2 men, 2 women—Interior

At its recent world premiere at the famed Actors Theatre of Louisville, this enticing new drama moved an audience of theatre professionals up off their seats and on to their feet to cheer. Mr. Tovatt has given us an insightful drama about what is happening to the small, family farm in America—and what this means for the future of the country. The scene is a farmhouse whose owners are on the verge of losing their farm. They are visited by their son and his wife, who live "only" eight hours' drive away. The son has a good job in the city, and his wife does, too. The son, Harry, is really put on the horns of a dilemma when he realizes that he is his folks' only hope. The old man can't go it alone anymore—and he needs his son. Pulling at him from the other side is his wife, who does not want to leave her job and uproot her family to become a farm wife. *Husbandry*, then, is ultimately about what it means to be a *husband*—both in the farm and in the family sense. *Variety* praised the "delicacy of Tovatt's dialogue", and called the play "a literate exploration of family responsibilities in a mobile society." Said *Time*: "The play simmers so gently for so long, as each potential confrontation is deflected with Chekhovian shrugs and silences, that when it boils into hostility it sears the audience."
(#10169)

CLARA'S PLAY
(LITTLE THEATRE—DRAMA)
By JOHN OLIVE

3 men, 1 woman—Exterior

Clara, an aging spinster, lives alone in a remote farmhouse. She is the last surviving member of one of the area's most prominent families. It is summer, 1915. Enter an immigrant, feisty soul named Sverre looking for a few days' work before moving on. But Clara's farm needs more than just a few days' work, and Sverre stays on to help Clara fix up and run the farm. It soon becomes clear unscrupulous local businessmen are bilking Clara out of money and hope to gain control of her property. Sverre agrees to stay on to help Clara keep her family's property. "A story of determination, loyalty. It has more than a measure of love, of resignation, of humor and loyalty."—Chicago Sun-Times. "A playwright of unusual sensitivity in delineating character and exploring human relationships." —Chicago Tribune. "Gracefully-written, with a real sense of place."—Village Voice. A recent success both at Chicago's fine Wisdom Bridge Theatre and at the Great American Play Festival of the world-reknowned Actors Theatre of Louisville; and, on tour, starring Jean Stapleton.
(#5076)

Other Publications for Your Interest

THE OCTETTE BRIDGE CLUB
(LITTLE THEATRE—COMIC DRAMA)

By P.J. BARRY

1 man, 8 women—Interior

There are no less than *eight wonderful roles for women* in this delightful sentimental comedy about American life in the 30's and 40's. On alternate Friday evenings, eight sisters meet to play bridge, gossip and generally entertain themselves. They are a group portrait right out of Norman Rockwell America. The first act takes place in 1934; the second act, ten years later, during a Hallowe'en costume/bridge party. Each sister acts out her character, climaxing with the youngest sister's hilarious belly dance as Salome. She, whom we have perceived in the first act as being somewhat emotionally distraught, has just gotten out of a sanitarium, and has realized that she must cut the bonds that have tied her to her smothering family and strike out on her own. This wonderful look at an American family in an era far more innocent and naive than our own was quite a standout at the Actors Theatre of Louisville Humana Festival of New American Plays. The play did not succeed with Broadway's jaded critics (which these days just may be a mark in its favor); but we truly believe it is a perfect play for Everybody Else; particularly, community theatres with hordes of good actresses clamoring for roles. "One of the most charming plays to come to the stage this season . . . a delightful, funny, moving glimpse of the sort of lives we are all familiar with—our own."—NY Daily News "Counterpunch".   (#17056)

BIG MAGGIE
(LITTLE THEATRE—DRAMA)

By JOHN B. KEANE

5 men, 6 women—Exterior/Interior

We are very proud to be making available for U.S. production the most popular play by one of contemporary Ireland's most beloved playwrights. The title character is the domineering mother of four wayward, grown-up children, each determined to go his own way, as Youth will do—and each likely headed in the wrong direction. Maggie has been burdened with a bibulous, womanizing husband. Now that he has died, though, she is free to exercise some control over the lives of herself and her family, much to the consternation of her children. Wonderful character parts abound in this tightly-constructed audience-pleaser, none finer than the role of Maggie—a gem of a part for a middle-aged actress! "The feminist awareness that informs the play gives it an intriguing texture, as we watch it unfold against a colorfully detailed background of contemporary rural Ireland. It is at times like hearing Ibsen with an Irish brogue."—WWD.   (#4637)

Other Publications for Your Interest

THE BALLAD OF SOAPY SMITH
(ADVANCED GROUPS—EPIC COMIC DRAMA)
By MICHAEL WELLER

24 men, 9 women (with doubling)—Various interiors and exteriors (may be unit set)

"Col." Jefferson Randolph Smith, known as "Soapy" to his friends and foes, is a celebrated, notorious con man whose reputation has, alas, not preceded him to the Alaska Gold Rush town of Skagway in 1897, when the play takes place. Soapy is a charming gentleman, and he starts up a protection racket which brings law and order to the town, giving it a church and an infirmary. Oddly enough Soapy, the criminal, becomes a force for moral good; until the town's hypocrisy and vicious self interest bring him down, a victim of the cardinal sin of believing in his own con. "Michael Weller deserves praise for a historical play with contemporary relevance, daring to accost a large canvas. The protagonist is a complex and absorbing creation. I left the theatre, for once, thinking rather than trying to forget."—N.Y. Mag. "A rousing epic"—AP. "A good time on a grand scale, with a mind and vision of rare intensity."—Gannett/Westchester Newsp. (#3975)

HURLYBURLY
(ADVANCED GROUPS—DRAMA)
By DAVID RABE

4 men, 3 women—Interior

This rivetting new drama by the author of *The Basic Training of Pavlo Hummel, Sticks and Bones* and *Streamers* took New York by storm in a production directed by Mike Nichols and starring William Hurt, Sigourney Weaver, Judith Ivey, Christopher Walken, Harvey Keitel and Jerry Stiller. Quite a cast, and quite a play! The drama is the story of four men nosedeep in the decadent, perverted, cocaine-laden culture that is Hollywood; pursuing their sex-crazed, dope-ridden vision of the American Dream. "*Hurlyburly* offers some of Mr. Rabe's most inventive and disturbing writing. At his impressive best, Mr. Rabe makes grim, ribald and surprisingly compassionate comedy out of the lies and rationalizations that allow his alienated men to keep functioning (if not feeling) in the fogs of lotusland. They work in an industry so corrupt that its only honest executives are those who openly admit that they lie."—N.Y. Times. "Rabe has written a strange, bitterly funny, self-indulgent, important play."—N.Y. Post. "An important work, masterly accomplished."—Time. "A powerful permanent contribution to American drama . . . rivetting, disturbing, fearsomely funny . . . has a savage sincerity and a crackling theatrical vitality. This deeply felt play deserves as wide an audience as possible."—Newsweek. (#10163)

Other Publications for Your Interest

THE CURATE SHAKESPEARE AS YOU LIKE IT
(LITTLE THEATRE—COMEDY)
By DON NIGRO

4 men, 3 women—Bare stage

This extremely unusual and original piece is subtitled: "The record of one company's attempt to perform the play by William Shakespeare". When the very prolific Mr. Nigro was asked by a professional theatre company to adapt *As You Like It* so that it could be performed by a company of seven he, of course, came up with a completely original play about a rag-tag group of players comprised of only seven actors led by a dotty old curate who nonetheless must present Shakespeare's play; and the dramatic interest, as well as the comedy, is in their hilarious attempts to impersonate all of Shakespeare's multitude of characters. The play has had numerous productions nationwide, all of which have come about through word of mouth. We are very pleased to make this "underground comic classic" widely available to theatre groups who like their comedy wide open and theatrical. (#5742)

SEASCAPE WITH SHARKS AND DANCER
(LITTLE THEATRE—DRAMA)
By DON NIGRO

1 man, 1 woman—Interior

This is a fine new play by an author of great talent and promise. We are very glad to be introducing Mr. Nigro's work to a wide audience with *Seascape With Sharks and Dancer*, which comes directly from a sold-out, critically acclaimed production at the world-famous Oregon Shakespeare Festival. The play is set in a beach bungalow. The young man who lives there has pulled a lost young woman from the ocean. Soon, she finds herself trapped in his life and torn between her need to come to rest somewhere and her certainty that all human relationships turn eventually into nightmares. The struggle between his tolerant and gently ironic approach to life and her strategy of suspicion and attack becomes a kind of war about love and creation which neither can afford to lose. In other words, this is quite an offbeat, wonderful love story. We would like to point out that the play also contains a wealth of excellent **monologue** and **scene material**. (#21060)